CW00740581

AC/DC AT 50

motorbooks

MARTIN POPOFF

CONTENTS

PART 3
LEGACY

PART 4
MALCOLM

INTRODUCTION

The challenge: to generate, present in chronological order, and then write about fifty AC/DC career highlights. This wasn't my idea but, rather, the brainchild of the good folks at Motorbooks. For my part, I instantly loved the idea, because any day writing about AC/DC is a good day in my books. Fact is, I'm on record all over the internet as calling AC/DC my favorite band of all time, although, granted, I'm usually quick to talk about ZZ Top, Deep Purple, Blue Öyster Cult, and even Max Webster as part of that gang, until I wind up conceding that it's a sort of five-way tie for first place.

Once I got down to the task, however, there were a few stumbling blocks, albeit minor ones. First off, there is an inherent difficulty in writing about AC/DC because they've always been quite a secretive, circle-the-wagons lot, with a self-imposed cone of silence around the Young brothers, including older brother George. There's also this vague suspicion in the industry that the cone of silence extends to the wider family, be it official through nondisclosure agreements or simply implicit. That might just be paranoia speaking, because it bleeds into the second difficulty: the fact that they never did a ton of interviews and, when they did, not much insight was revealed. It's a bit of a feedback loop: When you make a form of irresistibly and daringly simple music with simple lyrics, there's not much to talk about, so why bother talking? In other words, accusations of secrecy may be largely unwarranted. It might just be that the guys discovered early that it's not so easy to talk about AC/DC, which one might frame as abstract art, versus something like progressive rock, which is more "bitty", as they say, meaning there's lots more to jaw over.

And yet fortunately, the mandate of this celebration of a book wasn't one of unearthing underlying drama or particularly obscure factoids. It was more about those big, public career milestones, which for AC/DC, given their blinding success, were many. This brings up another salient point, however, upon which the air needs to be cleared: We've necessarily shifted the meaning of the word *highlight* away from the idea of strictly positive or successful to include tragedy and disappointment. In this respect, the entries that you're about to read represent more newsworthy moments along AC/DC's trajectory, ranging from diamond certifications to dementia and death. Again, these are essentially front-page stories culled from the band's wider narrative, I suppose "milestones," if again, as with the word *highlight*, you will allow the definition to include not-so-happy moments or even ones that are neutral, emotionally. Another way to look at this: All fifty of the topics unfurling over the following pages are highlights from the outside looking in, not always so happy for the boys in the band and often indeed not happy at all, but, to be sure, "beats" in an imagined TV or movie script one might cook up on the subject of the band.

And yes, I wrestled momentarily at the outset of including every studio album and indeed every live record and even the box sets as stand-alone entries. But then I got to thinking: For the guys in AC/DC, given the sort of shroud of mystery around their private lives, and given the enormity of fame they had foisted upon them, there's always been a distance. But it's a distance that is summarily eradicated by the brilliance of the band's charming, rootsy, people's music. Indeed, it's pretty much impossible to find anywhere in rock 'n' roll a body of work less pretentious than AC/DC's. In other words, despite the castle-keep nature of AC/DC, it's pretty easy to look at them as the best friends we've ever had simply by way of what they've given us with the records and the live shows. Ergo, the records and so many of the live shows have been singled out for exposition throughout these fifty entries.

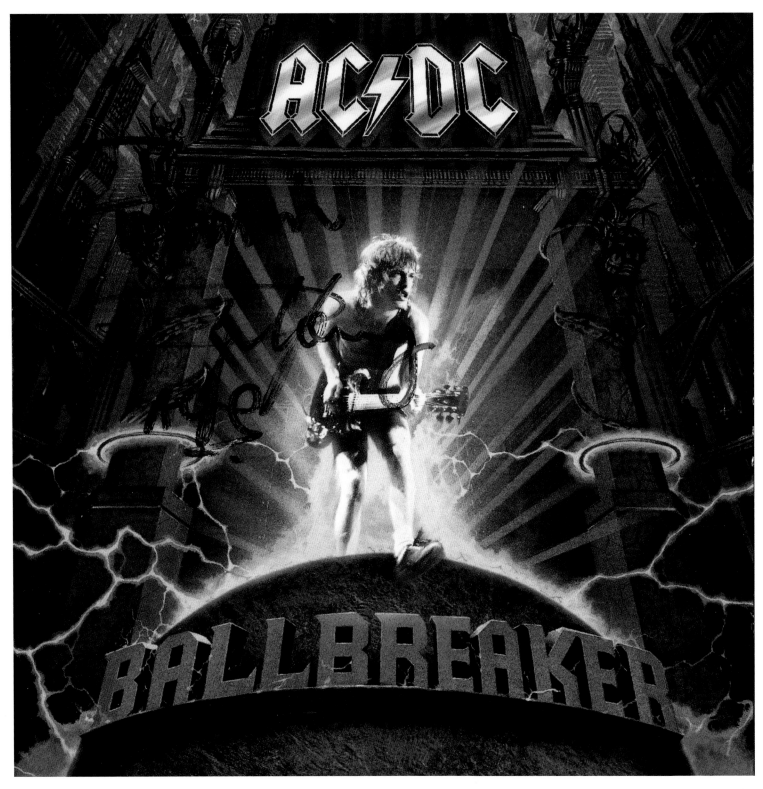

And if I may indulge for a few moments, here are a handful of highlights of my own interaction with the band (and to underscore the above point, most of these are about deep connection with the records themselves).

I remember first making the acquaintance of AC/DC's weirdly heavy '50s rock 'n' roll music at fourteen years old, buying *Let There Be Rock* in 1977 on a cross-country family vacation, specifically picking it up at Kelly's (a Canadian record and stereo chain) in Winnipeg, Manitoba. Then came *High Voltage* (purchased on the same trip), which marked a slight disappointment, given that it wasn't nearly as heavy as *Let There Be Rock*.

A super-giddy memory, higher than a kite over and above the two already cited, was the act of purchasing an import copy of *Dirty Deeds Done Dirt Cheap* via mail order out of one of those black-and-white, typed (in Courier font) with handwritten additions, photocopied (too many times), stapled, 5 1/2" x 8 1/2" catalogs stuffed with simple line listings (and the occasional five-word opinion) that would drive an angry young metalhead insane.

I remember eventually unsheathing the inner sleeve of *Dirty Deeds*, with the pictures of the band in a squalid dressing room and the black bars over their eyes, and thinking, are these guys some gang of crazy scary outlaws? And then once I heard the record, again, already thinking as much after owning *High Voltage* and *Let There Be Rock*, I found myself feeling weirdly sorry for them because of the obvious deficiency of IQ being demonstrated versus, for example, the band that brought us *Sad Wings of Destiny* and *Sin After Sin*. Somewhat sensibly, my fifteen-year-old buddies and I chalked this up to the fact that they were from Australia and didn't know better.

Then there's the recollection of scurrying home from the Kelly's in my hometown of Trail, British Columbia, on a hot summer day with *Powerage* bungee-corded to the back of my bike, hoping that it wouldn't melt during the course of the uphill, three-mile (4.8-km) sprint back to Glenmerry. It was fine, and (bonus), once past the cellophane, it turned out to be red vinyl.

My next fond memory was *Highway to Hell*, also jetted home from the Kelly's downtown on a hot summer day. I remember like it was yesterday, calling up my best buddy Forrest Toop and reporting to him on the album using our almost perfectly agreed-upon rating system for heaviness. For dramatic effect, I broke the rule and ran through the slightly less impressive side 2 first. This was because when I got around to side 1, the assessment was "average good" and then—*pow!*—"really good," "really good," "really good," "really good." That's about as perfect a side we ever had using our system. Incidentally, *Let There Be Rock* was only the second-ever "perfect" album we'd heard, after Rainbow's *Rising*, meaning there were only lousy goods, average goods, and really goods and no so-sos or lousys—next was the Sex Pistols album and the second Motörhead. But the biggest surprise was getting four "really goods" from a band that rarely delivered the top-shelf metal we got out of bands like Black Sabbath and Judas Priest, which, frankly, as stated above, we considered way smarter (and heavier).

The next fond memory comes from working my last three years in high school at Rock Island Tape Center, with boss Gordon Lee and the aforementioned Forrest Toop. How do AC/DC fit into this? Well, *Back in Black* was our favorite go-to stereo demonstration record, regularly cranked in the basement, helping us earn nice commissions as we sold stereos worth thousands of dollars to guys working "on the hill," namely the Cominco lead and zinc smelter, the town's largest employer. God love 'em, there was a constant parade of these fellas working there straight out of high school with money to burn. And burn it they did at our store on Klipsch, Bose, JBL, and Cerwin-Vega speakers powered by huge 160- and 200-watt Yamaha amps and receivers and occasionally the odd McIntosh, which usually wound up back in the shop for repairs. But yes, aiding in the cause was either the first full-band blast of "Back in Black" or conversely, the bells of "Hells Bells" and then what ensued.

The naivete and magic and freshness of youth now over—and really, with metal more routinely available courtesy of the New Wave of British Heavy Metal (NWOBHM) and beyond—my next and last big-deal AC/DC memory comes more than twenty years later when I got to interview Malcolm in person at the hotel the day after the huge Toronto Rocks concert. I got to say hi to Angus in the hallway (he was wearing the white hotel

housecoat and carrying a tray of tea), got a few things signed by him and Brian and Malcolm; but the best part was just sitting down with Malcolm for twenty minutes or so and speaking with this lovely man.

In any event, yes, sure, I have no problem calling AC/DC my favorite band of all time; and so it was an absolute joy celebrating their trials and tribulations, the emotional highs and the emotional lows experienced across an extraordinary career as one of the biggest bands of all time, and a "heavy metal" band to boot, meaning they were one of our own. To be sure—pick a spot, maybe somewhere around the middle of the 1980s—calling AC/DC a heavy metal band, given the intensifying evolution of the form, begins to feel a bit inaccurate. But we shouldn't lose sight that from the beginning through to *Flick of the Switch*, they were absolutely that. But from maybe a year or two or three after the release of *The Razors Edge*, when they stopped punching the clock regularly, that's when the legend had grown to the point where AC/DC became a genre unto itself, a self-defined part of the pop

culture fabric made up of at least two and possibly three personalities and icons among the ranks in Brian, Angus, and Malcolm. They had now become rock 'n' roll royalty, irrespective of what kind of music they played. In other words, AC/DC, just like Metallica a generation later, tricked regular people into liking heavy metal—and original old crusty metalheads like myself and all my buddies haven't been able to stop laughing about it since.

So there's the deal. That's who you've got on board the double-decker bus as guide and interpreter to the fifty AC/DC tourist attractions rocking to a Phil Rudd backbeat in the following pages. What emerges by the end, hopefully, is an appreciation of the enormity these guys accomplished from the utmost humblest of beginnings. And with that said, "Ride on."

PART 1
BONFIRE

Antipodean problem
children, circa 1976

01

PROBLEM CHILD:

AC/DC FORMS IN SYDNEY

Angus Young started smoking when he was eight, but after being bit hard once by the whiskey as a kid, he became a lifelong teetotaler. That's the AC/DC origins story in a nutshell, or at least in one of myriad legendary anecdotes, many of them borne of the type of cut-to-the-bone desperation that would get a kid on the tobacco well before he'd reach his maxed-out height of five foot two (157.5 cm).

William and Margaret Young had eight children spread over a twenty-two-year span, with Malcolm (born January 6, 1953) and Angus (born March 31, 1955) being the youngest, and all but one of the kids being boys. Life was constant poverty in Glasgow no matter how hard William worked. There was also the "big freeze" extreme winter of 1963, so the family decided to take advantage of an emigration program to Australia, which cost the family all of twenty British pounds.

Arriving in Sydney, the Youngs first lived in what was described as a tin hut. Fortunately, the family had music in its blood, most of the kids playing something, with older brother George finding surprise success in the trade with his band The Easybeats, and one of the brothers, in fact, staying behind in the United Kingdom due to his gig with Tony Sheridan. Watching George (and watching girls watching George) spurred Malcolm and Angus on, with the two quickly becoming advanced musicologists, buying as many records as they could afford and eventually seeing some landmark artists when they managed to

First studio
photo shoot,
1974

get to Sydney, including The Yardbirds, The Who, and the Small Faces. Angus also took his dad's wise advice to hit the library anytime he wanted to learn something, and there he found many issues of *Downbeat* magazine, where he learned even more about blues and jazz and their interfacing with rock. As for playing, Angus started on a banjo, followed by a used acoustic guitar his mom bought for him, en route to his first Gibson SG in 1970, when Angus had just quit high school at the age of fifteen.

Malcolm played in local bands such as Beelzebub Blues, Red House, and Rubberband, eventually stepping up to Velvet Underground (not the New York band), which got him out of Sydney for the first time. Angus would travel with the guys, picking up musician tips, eventually winding up in his own first band in 1972 called Kantuckee, which soon became Tantrum. Both Velvet Underground and Tantrum had extensive repertoires and played often, with the Youngs building the sort of muscle memory we attribute to The Beatles during their Hamburg era.

A further step up the career ladder came when rock star brother George and George's workmate Harry Vanda included them on the sessions for an album called *Tales of Old Grand-Daddy*, the one and only album to come from Vanda's and Young's post-Easybeats act, Marcus Hook Roll Band, issued through EMI locally in 1973. Meanwhile, Malcolm had decided to make his next musical venture, one that would include his younger brother, despite the fact that the two fought like brothers tended to do.

The name for the new act, formed in November 1973, would be inspired by the Youngs' sister, Margaret, who spotted "AC/DC"—standing for alternating current/direct current—on the back of her sewing machine. (Of note as well, one of Malcolm's many jobs after he was legally allowed to leave high school was repairing sewing

machines in a bra factory!) Augmenting the lineup of the newly minted AC/DC was Larry Van Kriedt on bass, Colin Burgess on drums, and Dave Evans on vocals. Band documents consider a December gig at *The Last Picture Show* the first AC/DC show ever, but most point to a New Year's Eve gig at Chequers at the very end of 1973 as the band's true coming-out party, with covers of Chuck Berry, The Beatles, and The Rolling Stones being on order to usher in 1974.

Early on the band had for themselves a haphazard and embarrassing sort of glam image, with little about the visuals messaging much more than "fashion disaster," save for Angus Young, who, once past experiments as Spider-Man, Superman, Zorro, and King Kong, finally settled upon the iconic schoolboy outfit that would have everybody talking about this precocious band of boogie-woogie upstarts.

02
LOVE AT FIRST FEEL:
DEBUT SINGLE, "CAN I SIT NEXT TO YOU, GIRL"

Fun stuff, trying to find the baby steps of the precocious school boy within the Marcus Hook Roll Band album, but they are indeed there, pulsing insistently on songs like "Quick Reaction," "Watch Her Do It Now," "Shot in the Head," "Natural Man," and "Louisiana Lady." But it's the stealth boogie shuffle of "Red Revolution" that we hear on AC/DC's first single, "Can I Sit Next to You, Girl," written by Malcolm and Angus and produced by George and Vanda, recorded at Albert Studios (where the duo were staff producers) and issued through Albert Productions on July 22, 1974.

By this point, the band had parted ways with original drummer Colin Burgess, landing upon Peter Clack after a stint with Ron Carpenter and Russell Coleman. However, even though Clack was in the band, playing in the video made for the song as well as subsequent live shows, it's Burgess who drums on the recording. There was a new plunker of the fat strings in the band as well, with Rob Bailey replacing Larry Van Kriedt. It was indeed Larry who had recorded the bass for the single, but his parts would be replaced by George.

Above and opposite:
Chequers, Sydney,
Australia, May 18, 1974

guitar solo from Angus. The last forty-five seconds of the song find everybody clanging away behind a gang vocal, and indeed we are in a place as squarely hard rock as any of the glam bands that AC/DC looked like were, circa this period back in the United Kingdom.

Over to the B-side and we have "Rockin' in the Parlour," a song that demonstrates less of the band's budding magic, coming off as a sort of louder, toughened-up T. Rex or David Bowie joint, slinky boogie rock but dated, lacking the sturdy framing we'd soon come to expect from Angus and Malcolm, with the latter in fact taking the solo on the song.

Now with a record out—there was also a release of the single in New Zealand, on Polydor—the band hit the tour trail, supporting Stevie Wright and, in late August, Lou Reed, who was on his first-ever visit to Australia, promoting *Sally Can't Dance*. The band showcased the song on an Australian TV show called *Countdown* and also made a professional promotional video for the track, miming it very accurately for the cameras on stage at *The Last Picture Show*. In the clip, one can see Angus in his schoolboy outfit, with the rest of the guys clad in typical glam garb, albeit toned down compared to what was happening on the other side of the world.

"Can I Sit Next to You, Girl" was deemed good enough for a revisit once the band got for themselves a new vocalist, with the song showing up on AC/DC's second full-length album, *T.N.T.* But indeed, all the ingredients were there back at the original, recorded capably by George and his equally experienced partner Vanda. The bad news is that the song stalled at #50 on August 26, 1974, on the local charts, while the good news is that AC/DC became a bit of a hot commodity in Perth and Adelaide, not the last territories they would conquer.

Dave Evans was still the band's vocalist at this point, despite his posting being wobbly, given repeated clashes with manager Dennis Laughlin, which culminated in a physical altercation at one point. Laughlin was the original singer for soon-to-be Aussie sensations Sherbet and would actually sub in for Dave from time to time.

But if "Can I Sit Next to You, Girl" had made it onto *Tales of Old Grand-Daddy*, it would have been the hardest-charging beast on that occasionally somewhat rocking record. Angus and Malcolm are at the fore with a stomping boogie that marries the heavy glam of Sweet and Slade and Mud to a Status Quo in transition, *Piledriver* and up, so to speak. But Angus also tosses in a bit of a circular, Celtic-sounding lick, raising the interest level. Dave sings the hell out of it, fronting the situation like a good front man should. There's also an early demonstration of AC/DC's patented "less is more" philosophy through a cutting back of the energy come chorus time, which lasts only momentarily until the tension rises, the question inherent in the song's title becoming rhetorical. There's even a built-in crowd participation version of the chorus, plus a typical-enough

03

ROCK 'N' ROLL SINGER:

BON SCOTT JOINS

Like Dave Evans, like Angus and like Malcolm, Ronald Belford "Bon" Scott was a product of emigration from the United Kingdom to Australia, having been born July 9, 1946, in Forfar, Scotland, part of a local government council area called Angus. Busted for a variety of offenses and rejected by the Australian Army as "socially maladjusted," Bon worked his way through odd jobs until he found his calling in rock 'n' roll, beginning his career in 1964 drumming for The Spektors, with whom he drummed and sang as the band banged out covers of The Kinks, The Beatles, The Pretty Things, and Them, featuring Van Morrison (even if Bon's idol was Little Richard). Bon had begun his life in music not as a singer but as a drummer, at the age of ten, when, having just moved with his family to Western Australia, he joined the Fremantle Scots Pipe Band.

After The Spektors came The Valentines, with whom Bon made his first record, in fact, featuring on a number of singles and a couple of EPs but no album. Bon actually got to tour the United Kingdom for the first time with his next band, a Grateful Dead-like psychedelic-cum-prog rock outfit called Fraternity, who recorded two full-length albums, *Livestock* in 1971 and *Flaming Galah* in 1972, both with Bon as lead vocalist of the band.

Once home from Britain, Fraternity went on hiatus, with Bon taking another job (at a fertilizer plant) while working on songs with a loose collective called the Mount Lofty Rangers. Next, in May 1974, Bon found himself in a coma after a drunken motorbike accident, which almost cost him the gig with this new band that was on the prowl for a new lead singer, called AC/DC. He'd been in a bad way beyond the coma, with many broken bones, his teeth smashed, and his jaw wired shut. A partially recovered Bon was suggested to George by Vince Lovegrove, Bon's co-lead vocalist from The Valentines. George already knew Bon, because The Valentines had recorded several songs that he had written.

The Valentines, circa 1969, with Bon Scott (second from left)

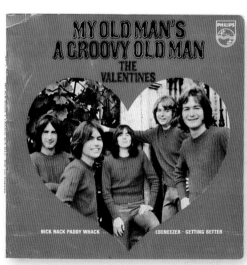

FRATERNITY

Livestock Fraternity

George, Malcolm, and Angus had a meeting with the recovering hard man. George was worried that Bon, three months older than he and seven years older than Malcolm, was "too old to rock," while Bon expressed concern that Malcolm and Angus were too young and inexperienced for his liking. But they held an all-night jam session, and Bon was in.

There are competing stories concerning Bon's hiring however, one involving the band's new manager, Michael Browning, who took the band on after witnessing their show at his venue called the Hard Rock Café, hiring Bon as the band's driver. Bon's wife, Irene Thornton, says that Bon simply jumped up on stage one night in September 1974 at the Pooraka Hotel when AC/DC were bluffing their way through an instrumental set after having just fired Dave Evans. Mixed in with this are stories of Bon's intention first to land a gig as the band's drummer.

What is pretty much agreed upon is that Bon joined AC/DC on October 24, 1974, and not as their drummer. To be sure, he was older than the other members, tattooed, a bit scary but charismatic, and definitely experienced, having been in serious bands for ten years at this point. Plus there was an instant connection given that both Bon and the Youngs had moved here from Scotland. And whatever the temporal sequence, Bon in fact did double as AC/DC's driver for a spell, as the band immediately started playing gigs, although very few, because mere days after Bon's hiring, the guys were in the studio making what was to be their debut album, *High Voltage.*

04
SHOW BUSINESS:
DEBUT ALBUM, *HIGH VOLTAGE*

Done the old-school way, AC/DC's first album was recorded quickly, between gigs, essentially live and with whomever could get the job done, whether they were in the band or not. *High Voltage*, issued February 11, 1975, on the Albert Productions label, found George Young running the show, in conjunction with his co-producer Harry Vanda, but with George and Malcolm sharing bass duties instead of band member Rob Bailey doing the honors. On drums was session musician Tony Currenti, subbing in for band member Peter Clack, who plays on only one track, the opener, a cover of "Baby, Please Don't Go." (A third drummer, John Proud, drums on "Little Lover.")

Albert Studios in Sydney was a nice place. It was spacious, but the band was tucked into a cramped corner of the complex and just bashed out these rudimentary songs live, with Angus and Malcolm divvying up lead guitar duties. The sessions lasted just two weeks in November 1974, with the band squeezing in a few gigs to stay fresh.

The original Australian *High Voltage* (more on the international version later) is the work of a band pretty much in possession of a sound, one that is to be retained and developed, save for essentially one track, "Love Song" (originally called "Fell in Love"). This marks the first and last time the bandmates would suggest a sincere ballad, even putting a level of decorum to the thing that we wouldn't see elsewhere on the album—"Love Song" wouldn't be out of place on a Fraternity album.

Perhaps also out of character is "Baby, Please Don't Go," incorrectly credited at first to Big Bill Broonzy and then in later pressings corrected to read Joe Williams. On the one hand, it serves as a blueprint for the band's own "Let There Be Rock"; but on the other hand, it's a cover, something AC/DC don't do moving forward, save for a Chuck Berry song on the second album. This was the first single from the record, most remembered in AC/DC lore for its performance on *Countdown*, where Bon is dressed as a schoolgirl.

The remaining six selections are all built like the AC/DC classics we all know and love—traditional, repetitive, rhythm guitars in Rolling Stones lockstep, equally spare bass, drums, and vocals—but roughly half of the songs equal the standard of a few tracks on the next two records, while the other half fall short. Of the seven tracks that are not covers, "Soul Stripper" is attributed to Malcolm and Angus, while all the rest include Bon in the credits.

Dispensing with the weak in the knobby knees, "Show Business" is an uneventful rote rocker (like "The Rocker"), "Little Lover" is a down-wound blues albeit with a bit of a riff to it, and "You Ain't Got a Hold on Me," well-written song that it is, lacks for guitars, oddly presaging an arrangement ethic repeatedly used in the 2000s.

Closer to the composite main style of the band as demonstrated through the catalog up to but not including *Let There Be Rock*, first we have "She's Got Balls," written about Bon's wife, Irene, who was Bon's rock during his recovery from his motorcycle accident. "Soul Stripper" (originally "Sunset Strip," written with Dave Evans) includes a little more percussion than we'll hear moving forward. Still, there are AC/DC tropes in development, including naked bass lines attacked by more and more guitars as the song builds. By the end, it's all hands on deck, with Malcolm taking an extended solo, cleaner of tone and more fluid than what we'd come to expect from Angus, and also firing off more structured licks than his younger brother. We'll hear more of this sort of song construction come "Squealer" from the third record.

Finally, there's "Stick Around," the most squarely AC/DC-like song on the album. Problem is, it's kinda dull; but then again, it's the work of a band daring us to consider the simple essence of rock 'n' roll, daring us to consider a song built of two chords and not much more than that come chorus time, maybe a couple more. The mind is forced to focus on a bass line that is a little busier than usual, taking up the slack, plus what Bon is saying. Also, maybe the band—well, George, too—is using simplicity to clear space for the forging of an opinion of Angus's guitar soloing on the track, which is laid-back but chock-full of the sort of rapid-fire bursts of the blues we'd expect from Angus moving forward.

Leaving this much space in the songs, as well as this level of blues and boogie predictability, turned out to be a stroke of genius, as the band found out playing all over Australia constantly in the months—all of them, right up to the making and baking of the next record—following the release of the album.

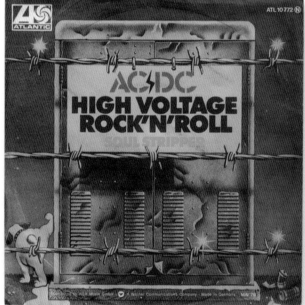

IT'S A LONG WAY TO THE TOP

(IF YOU WANNA ROCK 'N' ROLL)

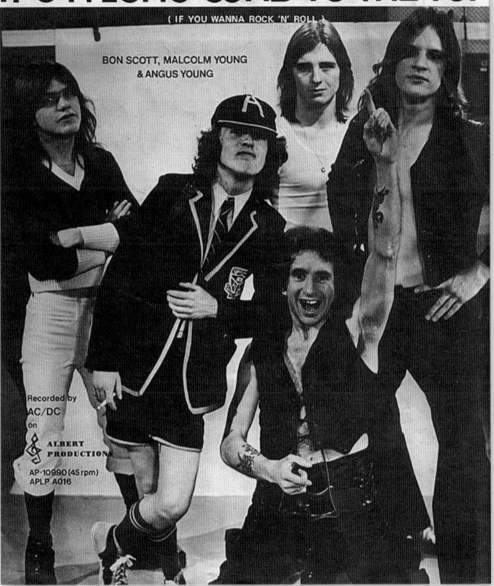

BON SCOTT, MALCOLM YOUNG
& ANGUS YOUNG

Recorded by
AC/DC
on
ALBERT
PRODUCTIONS
AP·10990 (45 rpm)
APLP A016

As Malcolm once told me, "The kids were just like that on the pub scene. Some of these pubs hold 1,500, 2,000; and they wanna rock out there. And the boogies, they could understand those straight enough. And we could boogie for half an hour—give 'em a boogie. It was like, 'Give us a boogie! Give us a boogie!' So everyone played a boogie. We used to like Canned Heat from way back, and we would just jam on stuff, around their ideas at the time, and we'd put a bit of boogie into our own material. But we were always into the blues and the rock 'n' roll stuff. We grew up on it. We had older brothers who were into Chuck Berry and Little Richard and Jerry Lee Lewis, and we grew up as kids hearing that. You know, it's in us. And we just tried to emulate that, these guys, with their feels, and get it really rockin' and then keep it going."

High Voltage turned out to be an instant success for the band, reaching #14 on the Australian charts and eventually climbing to five times platinum locally for sales of over 350,000 copies.

05

WAITING ROUND TO BE A MILLIONAIRE:
THE SECOND ALBUM, *T.N.T.*

There was no waiting around with AC/DC. With the first album just hitting the shops, the guys were soon back in Albert Studios plotting a follow-up, amid constant live (wire) gigging. A stand-alone single, pairing an electrifying new song called "High Voltage" with the swampy "Soul Stripper" from the first album, was issued June 23, 1975, whetting appetites for *T.N.T.*, which arrived (like the debut, only in Australia) December 1, 1975.

For the recording of "High Voltage" (along with the band's cover of Chuck Berry's "School Days"), George was still playing bass and Tony Currenti was still playing drums. However, once the band got into the studio, on and off between March and July 1975, there was a new rhythm section in town, namely Mark Evans on bass and Phil Rudd on drums. With this classic early-days lineup, the guys would refine their sound, to be sure, evident on the debut but now hammered home graphically on every song, save for outlier "The Jack." Still, ever important was George, who despite not being part of the credits, collaborated greatly with Malcolm in the formation of his and Angus's riffs into sensible songs, often composing on piano alongside Malcolm, who stuck with the guitar.

The beating heart of the *T.N.T.* album, the material to get excited about, comes with the likes of "It's a Long Way to the Top (If You Wanna Rock 'n' Roll)," "The Rock 'n' Roll Singer," "Live Wire," "T.N.T.," and "High Voltage." In effect, the last song on the debut, "Show Business," telegraphed a unified narrative across these tracks, because they are essentially all about the guys, collective or individually, and what it's like to be in a band, pertinently *this* band . . . of rogues.

Angus and Mal, Victoria Park, Sydney, September 7, 1975

Long way to the top:
Bon readies the
pipes, circa 1976.

So yes, essentially they're all about show business, with each one of these charmed accounts of life on the road being set to a musical track that is spare, atmospheric, and simmering, as the tension builds to a point of power at the end but intriguingly never too much of it. A rule book is adhered to, with nobody ever doing too much, most notably the drummer, although the riffs are never dressy either, nor are the bass lines. Conversely one might consider Bon's job normal, like that of singers in other bands. Then there's Angus (now the dedicated lead guitarist as Malcolm assumes his lifelong role as rhythm guitarist), who solos as often and as exuberantly as guitarists in other bands. But as for the rest of the presentation, as folks would soon regularly grouse, "easiest job in rock."

If there's a stylistic consistency to what's left, it's what we might call stomping boogie rock. The redo of the band's first single, "Can I Sit Next to You Girl" (no longer with the comma) aligns nicely with the Chuck Berry cover, which is made interesting—purposeful when it easily could have wilted as filler—by Bon's linguistic gymnastics. Then there's "Rocker," which is the same sort of thing sped up, played tightly but manic. This trio of songs—and for that matter the slow blues of "The Jack"—pay tribute to the band's heroes, while one could argue that the remaining five songs offer a modern style, one that is AC/DC's alone, at this point established to be reinterpreted, to be played with, on most of all the band's albums moving forward.

A pile of future concert staples began life right here on *T.N.T.*, as did Bon's amusing use of the bagpipes for the first couple of years. These can be heard on the first single "It's a Long Way to the Top," with the idea coming from George, who remembered that Bon had been in a pipe band, forgetting that he was a drummer there and knew nothing about the bagpipes. The legend of the pipes was further solidified when the band made a video for the track and included The Rats of Tobruk Pipe Band up on a flatbed truck with AC/DC as they rolled down Swanston Street in Melbourne. Add to this more appearances on *Countdown* and *T.N.T.* found itself vaulted to #2 on the Australian charts, eventually certifying as nine times platinum on home turf, the only place the album was ever issued (sorta).

06
LONG WAY TO THE TOP:

THE INTERNATIONAL COMPILATION VERSION OF *HIGH VOLTAGE*

AC/DC's second album was so important within the hallowed halls of rock 'n' roll, it wound up being a career highlight twice: once when it was released in Australia, making the guys beloved noisenik imps down under, and a second time when it was renamed *High Voltage* and sent out into the world.

Here is essentially what happened: The band signed a new worldwide record deal with Phil Carson out of the U.K. offices of Atlantic Records in November 1975, after which *T.N.T.* lost two tracks ("Rocker" and "School Days") but gained two others ("She's Got Balls" and "Little Lover") and got issued through the band's new agreement, confusingly, as *High Voltage*, on April 30, 1976, in the United Kingdom and two weeks later stateside.

Adding to the confusion, the United Kingdom, France, and Italy got one front wrapper, featuring a garish, neon-colored illustration of Bon and Angus, while the rest of Europe and North America got a sort of old-fashioned sepia-toned photograph of a young Angus with his tongue hanging out. Both covers at least suggested punk rock, the new and rebellious but equally basic music style squirming

to life at that exact time; and so both the press and the label's PR people sort of half-heartedly tried to portray the band as punks.

It might have been a good idea in terms of selling more records, because *High Voltage* didn't make much of an impression at the time. Fact is, at least in North America, on sleepy ATCO, it really wasn't marketed as much of anything. Additionally, at face value, AC/DC's music was daringly simple and, at this stage, not particularly heavy, something that would change come *Let There Be Rock*. So if you were a hard rock fan and dealt this particular platter, what you were hearing was a combination of Kiss and old-time rock 'n' roll.

In context, we'd already had Free, Cactus, and Mountain; and now we had Bad Company. But here's the thing: We'd also already had early Led Zeppelin, early Foghat, and early ZZ Top; and now we had the mature phases of those three bands, along with even more evolved properties like Ted Nugent and most notably Aerosmith, who, two weeks after *High Voltage* showed up in a handful of shops across the country, would issue a masterpiece called *Rocks*. And who made *Rocks*? America's Rolling Stones. And what were AC/DC? Australia's Rolling Stones. Only AC/DC were like the Stones from 1969 slightly turned up, and Aerosmith were nothing less than a high-technology full-blown replacement model, putting Mick and the rest of the band far in the rear-view mirror.

The point is that the handful of fans who bought *High Voltage* in America were sensibly not particularly moved. Bear in mind that AC/DC wouldn't play live in the United States until the summer of 1977. So all American kids had to go on was this collection of simple songs, a few funny things said by Bon on "She's Got Balls," and crotch-scratching stripper blues "The Jack," plus that fairly extreme voice of his and those amusing "ois" in "T.N.T." But other than that, this was the kind of music that would actually annoy critics, who, already smarting from the rise of Kiss, clearly couldn't wrap their heads around musicians who dared do so little musicianing.

That's exactly what I could figure out even at fourteen years old, with the complicating factor being that I had turned fourteen in April 1977, and, as explained in the introduction to this book, bought *Let There Be Rock* and *High Voltage* on the same cross-Canada family vacation. Once playing them in my bedroom back in British Columbia three weeks later, it was obvious the band had tripled the power on the "second" album, relegating the first, permanently for my buddies and me, as just politely tolerated. Felt sorry for, almost.

Consider this as well (especially if you were experiencing the record within that year before there was a *Let There Be Rock*): The album cover of *High Voltage* made it look like four of the guys in the band might be serving as supporting cast for some sort of child prodigy or, worse, idiot savant. It looked a little silly, or a little punk, or a combination of both. But then again, they're hicks from Australia, so give 'em a break—they can't possibly be ready to compete on the big stage. That's the problem: AC/DC most definitely could, and that's where these small songs exploded—on stage. Delivered loud and almost epileptic in a sweaty club, the *High Voltage* songs in fact sounded as bold and brassy as anything off the next three records. But the album wasn't to be toured stateside, so who knew?

Below and opposite: In London on the band`s first U.K. tour, May 1976

07
LIVE WIRE

FIRST DATES OUTSIDE AUSTRALIA

Angus and Bon onstage at the Marquee Club, London, May 12, 1976.

The death of Paul Kossoff, March 19, 1976, ex-of-Free and then with Back Street Crawler, on a cross-country flight in America, would cause big consequences in the careers of Sweet and Sammy Hagar. But those are stories for another time.

Kossoff's death would also have ramifications for AC/DC. The band had arrived in London, April 1, 1976, flying high after completing their third album, *Dirty Deeds Done Dirt Cheap*, and ready to go on tour supporting Back Street Crawler. With the legendary blues-rock guitarist gone, their plans were dashed and the guys were put up in an apartment at 49 Inverness Terrace, Bayswater, while a new course of action was put in place. In the meantime, three days later, Bon was in a pub he used to frequent with Fraternity and promptly got into a bar fight, dislocating his jaw and losing a few teeth, with a much-missed $2,000 spent to fix him up.

Three weeks later a gig was scheduled for Friday, April 23, at an establishment at 157 Hammersmith Row, West London, called the Red Cow, a pub with a venue in the back for 250 punters. The pay packet for the night was £35 and the band was scheduled for two sets. They were hellbent for leather from the start, first playing to a crowd of thirty, with Angus not skimping on his best bits, including soloing up on a roadie's shoulders and his fit bit collapsed upon the stage.

Mark Evans (right), Angus (rear), and Malcolm (front right) cool off backstage at the Marquee, August 9, 1976

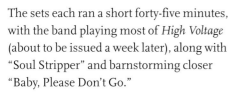

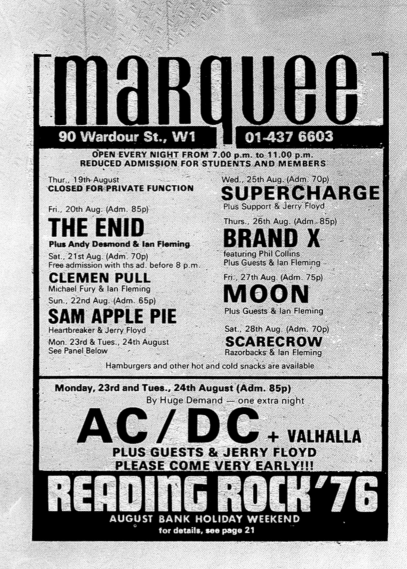

The sets each ran a short forty-five minutes, with the band playing most of *High Voltage* (about to be issued a week later), along with "Soul Stripper" and barnstorming closer "Baby, Please Don't Go."

After the first set the place cleared out, with the guys worrying that there'd be even fewer people for the second go-around. Turns out that witnesses had scurried to the phone booths to call their buddies down to catch the second set, and by various reports the place was somewhere between packed to double-full for set two. Once done, the band's U.K. booking agent, Richard Griffiths, told the guys, "That was the loudest, meanest thing I've ever heard in my life." As importantly, the band had made an impact with the locals, who had been fed as of late this new thing called punk rock plus various forms of a curious

music at the time called pub rock, which ranged from a sort of California country rock at the relaxed end to Dr. Feelgood and Eddie and the Hot Rods, and up into the vicinity at which AC/DC operated.

The band played the Red Cow the next night, then on April 26, the Nashville Rooms, more of a punk venue at the time, followed by a short residency at the Marquee. *Melody Maker*, *Sounds*, and *NME* all said kind things about the band as they set off on the *Lock Up Your Daughters* tour proper, in fact supporting a lesser version of Back Street Crawler, now called Crawler, with If's Geoff Whitehorn

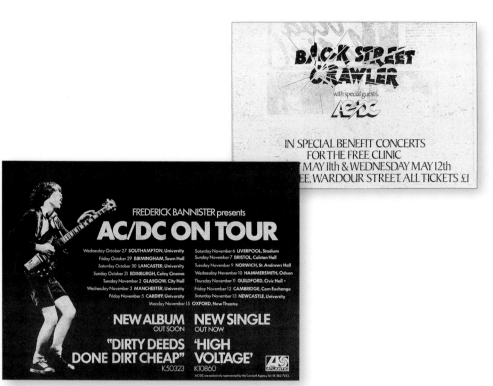

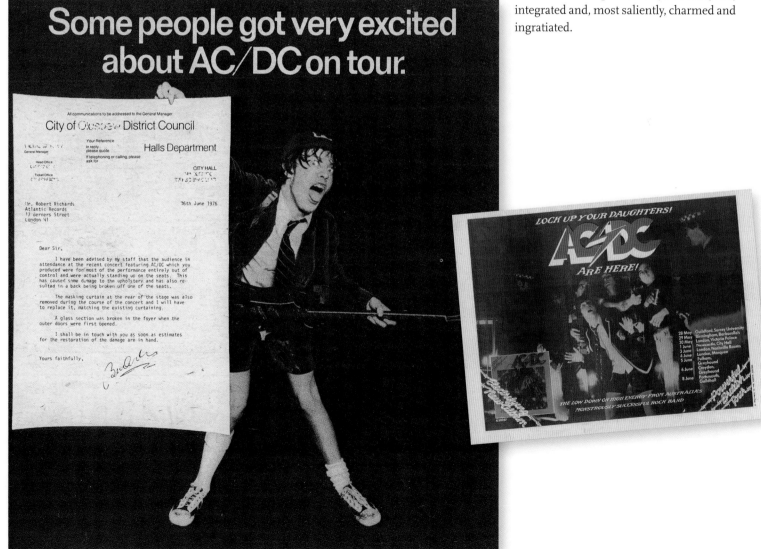

replacing Kossoff. The guys were positively swaggering, evidenced by an on-the-street interview in July in which Bon responded to a mention of The Beatles and The Rolling Stones by chuckling, "We're better. Who needs them? They're sort of last year's model."

By this point AC/DC had established their beachhead in the West, essentially relocating to the U.K. They'd played dozens of gigs through May, June, and July up and down the country. With but a week to sort it out, they were then off to Sweden and the rest of Europe, with dates back at the Marquee in London marbled in between, the venue becoming their new homestand right at the heart of the world's premier music city.

But the highlight would be the band's first time playing Reading, performing on the last night, Sunday, August 29. The European campaign continued all the way through to October of that year; by then AC/DC had not so much conquered but (to be sure) fully integrated and, most saliently, charmed and ingratiated.

08

GONNA BE SOME ROCKIN':

THE THIRD AUSTRALIAN ALBUM, *DIRTY DEEDS DONE DIRT CHEAP*

Presented with *Dirty Deeds Done Dirt Cheap*, Phil Carson had to do some backpedaling. It seems that his bosses at Atlantic didn't like the album and wanted to drop the band, which Carson managed to stave off, even if the record were not to be issued in North America (until 1981, but more on that later), a shocking setback for the band. Also aiding his argument was the fact that *High Voltage* had done acceptable business, especially against the fact that the album only cost $25,000 to make.

As for the label's concerns, there were complaints with the production of the record and even Bon's vocals on it, to the point where there was talk of Bon getting fired. Apparently they thought that it was hard to understand what Bon was saying, and it would certainly be worse in America, hence the suspension of the album's launch stateside. Indeed *Dirty Deeds* had been recorded in a rush, during a particularly busy period for the guys on the eve of leaving for halfway 'round the world, a long way from home and, it seems, for a long, long time.

The release of the third AC/DC album was couched in confusion typical for the band. For a front cover, Australia got a scrappy illustration of Bon and Angus playing pool. Europe got an artsy sleeve designed by the iconic Hipgnosis graphics house, but it wasn't a great example of the company's usually refined work and it was too intellectual set against the music enclosed. What's more, the versions differed by two swapped tracks. The Australian issue included "R.I.P. (Rock in Peace)" and "Jailbreak" (both not great), while the European version included "Rocker" from the Australian *T.N.T.* and "Love at First Feel," the first of only two songs ever not included on one of the Australian albums.

I'm not hearing the proposed problem with Bon's vocals, neither in his performance, which is typically lovable and carousing, nor his enunciation of the words. But there's a sense that the album marks no big improvement over *T.N.T./High Voltage*. Focusing on the international version, where the stakes were higher, "Rocker," "There's Gonna Be Some Rockin'," and "Squealer" are pretty much filler, while "Ride On" is another one of the band's slow blues, musically uneventful, even if it's quite a beloved track given Bon's world-weary lyric and gauzy, night-prowling vocal performance.

Elsewhere there's "Big Balls," which again sets a good lyric—this time mischievous and amusing, centred on a lascivious sexual double entendre—against music that is, alas, underwhelming. Still, that leaves four stomping, utilitarian AC/DC anthems as good as anything previously issued. "Problem Child" is simple, spacious, and almost poppy, evidently deemed good enough to be included on the international version of *Let There Be Rock*. "Ain't No Fun (Waiting Round to Be a Millionaire)" is an infectious upscale boogie rocker that includes a rare four-letter word from Bon. Australia made up for "Love at First Feel" not being on the record back home by issuing it as a single, backed with "Problem Child." It's not much to look at, but it's fun enough, a boogie but not rote, more of an unassuming, low-on-ambition Status Quo number, but with a bonus eye-wink from Bon.

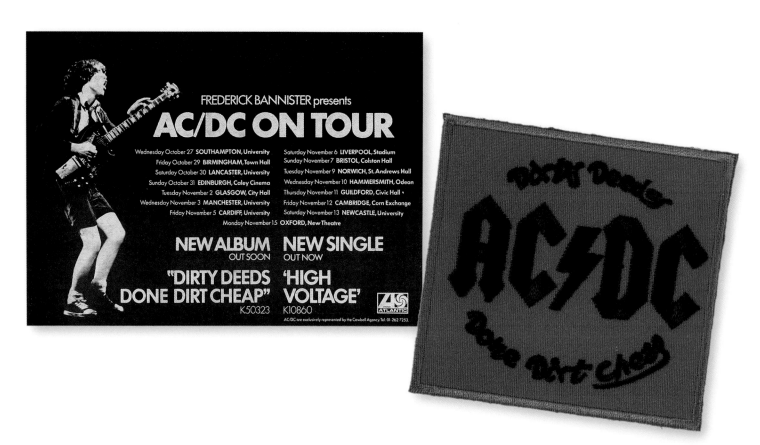

This leaves the title track, a classic forevermore, framed not much sturdier than "T.N.T." but just that little bit more exciting come chorus time. Plus the lyric tells a great story (indeed the whole album was loosely planned as a bit of a concept record, inspired by film noir Humphrey Bogart movies). The song pays tribute to a character called Dishonest John from the *Beany and Cecil* cartoon that Angus used to watch as a kid, who had for himself a business card stating, "Dirty deeds done dirt cheap. Special rates for Sundays and holidays." The phone number that Bon cites in the song was an actual Australian phone number. This caused problems once the album was released in the United States in 1981. During the song's break section, after Bon rattles off the number, he exclaims, "Hey!," which listeners in America interpreted as an eight. This completed a phone number in Libertyville, Illinois, prompting the owners of it to sue due to the harassment they were getting, along with, presumably, offers of employment.

Outside Shepperton Studios,
Surrey, U.K., 1976

Is *Dirty Deeds Done Dirt Cheap* an AC/DC
career highlight? Only inasmuch as it was
the band's third full-length album (as well
as the first on which the band wrote every
song). In fact, the record almost serves as a
setback, although if there's a silver lining to
be acknowledged, its ill reception resulted in
the rethink that brought us *Let There Be Rock*,
a resounding righting of the ship after which
there would be no looking back.

09
BAD BOY BOOGIE:
THE FOURTH ALBUM, *LET THERE BE ROCK*

Electronic distortion, tube amp distortion, solid state distortion, preamp distortion, preamp gain, clipping, overloaded microphones, overloaded consoles or just simple abuse and subsequent overheating of old and grimy amplifiers . . . there are many theories as to why *Let There Be Rock* (issued March 21, 1977, in Australia and July 25, 1977, internationally) sounds so fizzy, raw, and electric. These conjectures all come to light because the band swears up and down that no effects were used, with some combination of the above substituting for an effect, giving AC/DC the most power-packed production presentation they would ever propose.

As I once said to Malcolm, the guitars sound like chainsaws, to which he said, "That's right! Well, that was the idea. We thought with *Let There Be Rock*, we needed some new stage material; that's how we looked at it. We wanted to get the kids up more with it, get tougher." Which I suppose makes a different point, one I've read elsewhere as well—this idea that now having toured extensively in the United Kingdom and all over Europe, the band was hot and hungry for material that would drive the fans crazy, having now learned which of the old songs worked to that effect and which ones didn't.

A by-product of that touring as well was the fact that they were just getting to be better and better performers,

with Bon ending up even more histrionic on the new album, Phil Rudd pounding on the hoodlum rock four-on-the-floor, and Angus cutting and slashing his way through his guitar solos. Angus, in fact, cites this record as his favorite from that standpoint, lauding how guitar-centric it turned out. As for the construction, they didn't really do anything different, working once again with Harry Vanda and George, recording at Albert and recording quickly, writing on the spot, not making demos, locking in until they found a groove and then hitting the record button, with no click tracks and, like I say, no effects.

But back to the songwriting: *Let There Be Rock* is heavy from start to finish, almost oppressive, made more so by the scratch and distortion of the guitars, which are then placed loud in the mix, overwhelming the bass, drums, and vocals. Quantitatively, the songs are perhaps bluesier but also darker, less whimsical, more often locked into the plodding doom side of the blues, and then

almost thrashing when it comes to "Whole Lotta Rosie" and the title track.

The fast ones are the most famous songs on the record. "Let There Be Rock" is interesting because on it, Bon tells the story of rock 'n' roll couched in religious language. It's also quite the epic as well, and it's definitely one that showcases Angus at his manic best, evangelizing as feverishly on his axe as Bon does at the mic. This is also the song with the apocryphal story that had Angus wailing away at his guitar solo while smoke and sparks started shooting out of his amplifier, George egging him on, Angus literally playing with fire. As alluded to, this tale might also explain why the record sounds so fuzzy and buzzy, so headache-inducing—AC/DC were just beating the hell out of their equipment, perhaps subconsciously still smarting at Atlantic's decision not to put out *Dirty Deeds*, with the intent to deliver a record that would essentially bully the label brass into submission.

Back to the songs, "Whole Lotta Rosie" is interesting because it's the story of Bon getting with a groupie back home that was more than just a little overweight, which gave the band something to snicker about in interviews as the story grew and grew along with Rosie herself, each telling upon the next. At the music end, this one is a wall of sound, serving as a metaphor for the way fans would view the record as a whole moving forward. Elsewhere there was "Hell Ain't a Bad Place to Be," which would become a concert opener for years, while "Problem Child," a replacement for the Australian edition's "Crabsody in Blue," is simply irresistible, as Robert Palmer used to say.

"Dog Eat Dog" was a concert favorite as well, but as we drill down into the deeper album tracks, they all just beat the listener about the head, neck, and upper chest area, in creation of an album that could not be denied. And it wasn't. Fortunately for the band and for Atlantic, again, *Let There Be Rock* would be the second AC/DC album issued in America, the variation being the one swapped track as well as a better album cover, basically a pretty darned average live shot, instead of what we saw on the drab Australian issue, which gave us a black-and-white picture of some hands—owned by guitarist Chris Turner from Australia's original hard rock legends, Buffalo—on a fret board, blurry, framed by pretty basic type. In fact, there's a key difference as well: the international version of this record was the first to feature the Gerard Huerta-designed AC/DC logo that is one of the most recognized in rock to this day.

At the commercial end of things, it's not that *Let There Be Rock* was a big hit anywhere; it's more that it was so nasty that AC/DC could no longer be ignored. In that respect, it's almost like a piece of press gave the band notoriety, even if it wasn't selling like hotcakes. But it also gave the band an overhauled set list which, drawn and quartered live, also acted as a form of press or testimonial.

As for chart performance, AC/DC were still stars back home, with the album reaching #19 in the local charts. They were also able to hit #9 in France and #17 in the United Kingdom, while chart placement in the United States was less impressive, with the album stalling at #154 on the Billboard grid. But yes, in addition to my abstract notions about the record itself and the live show acting like press, there was proper traditional press, with AC/DC getting some of the best reviews of their career. And even when the reviews weren't particularly positive, they lacked any sense of ridicule, for indeed, *Let There Be Rock* was a serious record with a palpable sense of menace.

Wired for sound, save for the soon to be ousted Mark Evans (upper left).

10

GIMME A BULLET:

CLIFF WILLIAMS REPLACES MARK EVANS ON BASS

So typical and actually intriguing of the AC/DC camp, the reasons for the sacking of Mark Evans, whether you listen to Mark or Angus, has been kept considerably diplomatic. From Mark you get a sense of good riddance, hinting that the two didn't get along; and from Angus you get the feeling that he didn't think Mark was disciplined enough and that they wanted a more experienced bassist, perhaps one that could provide backup vocals. Then there was booking agent Richard Griffiths, who mused that, "You knew Mark wasn't going to last; he was just too much of a nice guy." Whatever the reason, Mark had bowed out after a show in Gothenburg, Sweden, supporting Black Sabbath, April 22, with two further Scandinavian dates getting canceled.

Enter Cliff Williams, an Englishman who Angus quipped was hired for his good looks and therefore his ability to attract more women to the gigs, along with the fact that he indeed passed an audition process (four jam sessions!), which wasn't surprising given his past with recording artists Home and Bandit, with five albums between them. I suppose this counts as an AC/DC milestone because Cliff was around for the duration of the band's blessed run, important to the situation for his Malc-like haircut and stage stance even if he'd never get brought into the writing cabal (not that he wrote a lick with Home or Bandit either). In addition, at five foot six (167.6 cm), Cliff was clocking in not very tall and second tallest in the band after Bon, keeping things compact.

In retrospect, despite all the drummers that AC/DC had gone through, the hiring of Phil Rudd should be considered a milestone as well. His long tenure in the band might have been similarly expected, given his past with two iconic acts from Australia's hard rock story, namely Buster Brown and Coloured Balls. Together the two made beautiful music together, forming a legendary rhythm section of utter simplicity, with Cliff—27 years old at the time when Mark had been but 21—officially hired May 27, 1977, and in fact playing his first gigs with the band in Australia, low-key to break him in, at Bondi Lifesaver in Sydney in early July.

There were a few snags getting his visa sorted—previous to Cliff, work papers had also been an issue with respect to AC/DC's delayed appearance on American soil—but once figured out, AC/DC had their first proper foreigner in the band. Significantly, Cliff certainly wouldn't be the last, with AC/DC proving to be perfectly happy to hire outside of Australia, in the process reconnecting with their English roots in pursuit of the perfect configuration to make this thing happen and happen big (but not tall).

HOME make unique soft rock sounds on their first album. Don't just take our word for it. Dial 01-493 7232 and hear for yourself (between Aug. 30th and Sept. 6th).
CBS 64356

MUSIC OF OUR TIME FROM THE MUSIC PEOPLE

CBS

HOME-The Alchemist

At the end of 1972 four out of five major music weeklies voted Home 'The Most Promising New Group For 1973'.

An award brought about by consistently good live performances and the release of two fine albums.

Now there is the third Home album: 'The Alchemist'.

Home make good again

Home: Mick Stubbs, Cliff Williams, Mick Cook and Laurie Wisefield. 'The Alchemist' Their new album on CBS 65550.

HOME | The Alchemist

the music people on records and tapes.

Cliff Williams performing in London with his band Home, January 20, 1974

11
FIRST BLOOD:
THE FIRST U.S. SHOWS

America beckoned, but first point of business: Break in the new bassist. As mentioned, this took place back at Bondi Lifesaver in Sydney, with AC/DC playing incognito (as The Seedies and then Dirty Deeds), with Rose Tattoo supporting and, fortunately, Cliff Williams passing the test.

Arriving in the United States, the band played their first show at the Armadillo World Headquarters in Austin, Texas, July 27, 1977, supporting regional breakout hit Moxy, who nonetheless were from a world away, namely Toronto, Canada. Attendance was pegged at about 1,500 fans paying $5 a head. As guitarist Earl Johnson told me, "In Texas it was like we got off the plane and had been The Beatles or something. We play Toronto all the time and the managers are all telling us to turn it down and they're going to fire us and everything, and you go down there and you get off the plane and you're The Beatles. They were playing full sides of our albums on the radio down there, not just the song. I remember to this day, we were playing a club with AC/DC, and I remember removing Bon Scott from my bed, throwing him over my shoulder, carrying him down the hall, and putting him in his own room. And I don't think that I even talked to the guy [laughs]."

Texas was known for being up on their obscure hard rock, with San Antonio being the American headquarters of heavy metal at the time thanks to headbanging disc jockey Joe Anthony. Other success stories there include Triumph, Saxon, and Budgie. The promoter of the show, Stone City Attractions' Jack Orbin, had heard AC/DC on radio thanks to Anthony and was intrigued. He managed to book the band for four Texas dates at $1,000 apiece.

Phil seen during a three-night stand at The Whisky a Go Go in Los Angeles, August 1977.

The Whisky a Go Go in Los Angeles, August 1977

Angus makes some noise at the band's first ever New York City show, at the Palladium, August 24, 1977.

Earlier on the night of that first show in Austin, rest assured AC/DC would have been taking care of business, playing a short set that featured dependable staples like "The Jack" and "Baby, Please Don't Go," but also new songs like "Dog Eat Dog," "Problem Child," and "Whole Lotta Rosie" from *Let There Be Rock*, issued just three days earlier. Filling out the set were the opening one-two punch of "Live Wire" and "She's Got Balls," both from the first record the band had out in America, *High Voltage*.

By some accounts AC/DC stole the show, but then again, Moxy had Buzz Shearman howling away up front and were no slouches (Shearman was a candidate to replace Bon Scott after Bon's death; Buzz himself would die in a motorcycle crash in 1983). AC/DC made enough of an impression that the next time back they'd be headlining Austin's Opry House (co-owned by Willie Nelson) to about the same-sized crowd, supported by San Francisco's Yesterday and Today, who had two records out by that point. It was due in large part to the success of the band's 1977 Texas stand, as well as the Florida and Midwest shows that followed, that Atlantic kept AC/DC on the roster to fight another day.

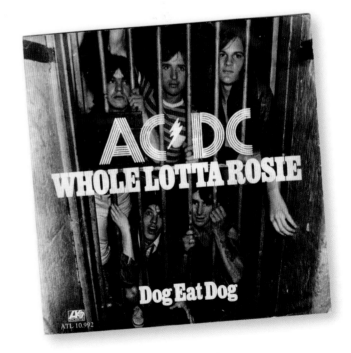

12
SAFE IN NEW YORK CITY

AC/DC PLAYS CBGB

It was the hot and trashy summer of 1977. Serial killer Son of Sam had just been arrested two weeks earlier and now it was time to party. Not that rock 'n' roll had stopped anyway, but on August 24, 1977, the Dictators were doing what they do, headlining to a sold-out crowd at the 3,400-capacity Palladium on 14th Street, supported by the Michael Stanley Band, taking the stage after opener AC/DC—all for $3.50.

Two things are significant here. AC/DC put on a rousing show, playing their short set of seven songs (depending on how you count) with those in attendance remembering Angus on a roadie's shoulders knocking out a great solo. The other significant factor is that the Dictators were a band smashing heavy metal into punk rock.

They would be joined by AC/DC in that battle of the pits, as the feisty, sweat-drenched support act headed over to New York punk Central, namely Hilly Kristal's CBGB dive, later that night to put on an impromptu set. Uninvited and just showing up, AC/DC played after the last band of the night, the Marbles, vacated the stage. AC/DC had already been riding this razor's edge, playing next to the punks back in their new headquarters, London, and dealing with record label folks who took one look at Angus and then at titles like "She's Got Balls," and thought they'd market AC/DC as a new punk band from Australia. But Malcolm and Angus were having none of that, knowing their genre-defying value and indeed knowing the value of the good and the bad within the punk scene.

Was heading down to CBGB more a case of curiosity? A case of checking out the competition? Checking out where the action was? Knowing the band's cocksure confidence, it was probably more a case of rising to the challenge of converting a demanding New York punk crowd into AC/DC fans. If these Lower East Side music snobs could only hear the power and the glory of point-blank rock 'n' roll, surely they would let down their defenses and surrender.

As the Marbles politely said good night and AC/DC slowly got it together, they would soon realize that the CBGB crowd was like any other: equally curious, appreciative, and willing to buy what AC/DC was selling. It was hot outside and even hotter inside, and the band was loud. Bon was in his tight blue jeans with matching blue jean vest which he quickly doffed. Methodically, in no hurry, the band proceeded to stack up the chords that became "Live Wire," followed by a similarly extended version of "She's Got Balls." By most accounts, after that it was the same songs that closed out the short set earlier in the evening at the Palladium, namely "Problem Child," "The Jack," "High Voltage," "Whole Lotta Rosie," and the band's manic cover of "Baby, Please Don't Go"—punk from a different time and space.

AC/DC would soon be back headlining the Palladium, playing there once in the summer of each of the following three years. As punk got increasingly politically, culturally, and visually defined and segmented, any hype concerning AC/DC as the new punks from Australia disappeared. Good riddance, sez Mal.

Photographer Robert Francos was fortunate to capture the band`s impromptu set at New York City`s legendary CBGB on August 24, 1977

13

DECIBEL:
AC/DC ISSUE
POWERAGE

Having worked in new bassist Cliff Williams like an old baseball glove, AC/DC converged once again on Albert Studios in Sydney with George and Vanda, cranking out their fifth record over three weeks of sessions, because, says Cliff, that's all the money they had. Issued May 5, 1978, pretty much simultaneously in all markets, *Powerage* nonetheless sported some differences depending on where you bought it. Mostly there were minor alterations in the mixes of certain songs—little details added, others missing—but a key difference would be the inclusion of an extra track, "Cold Hearted Man," on the European version. In addition, some early issues were rushed out, leaving off late arrival "Rock 'n' Roll Damnation."

Cooked up because the label was concerned there was no clear choice for a potentially successful single on the record, "Rock 'n' Roll Damnation" would indeed take care of that, being one of the poppier songs the band had written to date, with maracas and handclaps added and really no usual guitar solo section to speak of. Come chorus time, the song takes on a somewhat southern rock melody, which then carries over to the vibe of other songs on the record, the end result being that *Powerage* would sound more relaxed and organic, less halting and serious at the guitar position versus *Let There Be Rock*, but more reflective and ruminating when it came to Bon's world-weary lyrics. "Rock 'n' Roll Damnation," issued as an advance single, saw adequate radio play in North America and managed a #24 placement on the U.K. charts.

The band returns triumphant to New York's Palladium, August 24, 1978

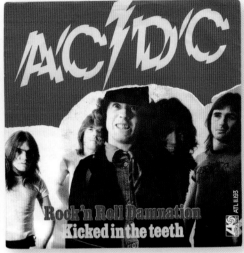

Indeed *casual* might be a good word for *Powerage*, as would be *charming*—inviting even—with songs like "What's Next to the Moon," "Down Payment Blues," "Gone Shootin'," and, to a lesser extent, "Gimme a Bullet" all being quieter arrangements than anything on the almost-menacing *Let There Be Rock* record.

At the heavy end, the note-dense and up-tempo "Riff Raff" would become a long-standing concert staple, while the comparatively grim "Sin City" would score as a minor hit from the album. Closing the record are two peas in a pod, "Up to My Neck in You" and "Kicked in the Teeth," which found the band rocking hard but simple of ambition. These tracks evoked the mischief-making adolescent songwriting of the *T.N.T.* album but with the heaviness of *Let There Be Rock*, if not that record's white-hot and redlined production values. (And speaking of teeth, it was in 1978 that Angus treated himself to a whole new set.)

Powerage is famously Keith Richards's favorite AC/DC album and, really, his entry point into an appreciation of the band; but it is also many a deep fan's pick—myself included, as I once mentioned to Malcolm, who agreed

that it was his favorite, too. Indeed, one might frame *Powerage* as the last magic moment in time before the band got self-aware and overly professional—George and Vanda would be replaced by Robert John "Mutt" Lange on the next record. It was also the first where they sound fully comfortable in their own skins, not out to please or, more pointedly, not concerned with being called the wildest, heaviest band on the circuit.

The end result was that AC/DC didn't particularly gain fans or lose them, with *Powerage*, after stalling at #133 on Billboard, having to wait until *Back in Black* had been out a full year before receiving its gold record certification. What's even more puzzling is that platinum certification did not arrive until 1990, with the record now thirty years hence still stuck at single platinum status. This happenstance indeed belies a record that is considered a dark horse of the catalog, regularly forgotten but also aptly called underrated, fitting that definition given the fact that, again, for many of the lifelong faithful, it's often cited as the greatest AC/DC album of all time.

HIGHWAY TO NOWHERE

AC/DC's rise to prominence took place during the final years with Bon Scott, a magical time marked by the *Powerage* album, followed by a live album, followed by *Highway to Hell* before Brian takes over for *Back in Black*. Curiously, all three feature on their front covers an embellished Angus. On *Powerage*, it looks like he's being electrocuted, with his hands replaced by electrical cables. On *If You Want Blood* he's being gored by a guitar, and on *Highway to Hell*, he's transformed into a devil. All three covers are art-directed by Bob Defrin, photographed by Jim Houghton with his business partner Earl Steinbicker assisting. What's curious, first off, is that an image from the *Powerage* photo shoot was used for the front cover of *Highway to Hell* a year later.

"Yes," explains Steinbicker, "the one with the horns. That had been taken previously. The one that we did out on the highway there, the night shot, really wasn't very dramatic, and so they decided to use this earlier picture for the cover. For *Highway to Hell*, we thought we'd be able to use our new shoot. We took them out on a deserted highway late at night and we set up lights and so forth, but somehow it didn't impress, and we used that on the back cover."

"There was a highway that was under construction on Staten Island, called the West Shore Expressway," continues Earl, "and we drove out there. We had this all set up with the city where they blocked it off for us, and we came out with a Honda generator truck for lights and had a smoke generator and so on. I remember we rode out there in a location van, which is a thing with dressing rooms; it's like a motor home. And they were so thrilled, because you could see all of New York. We drove across the Verrazzano-Narrows Bridge and you could see the whole city laid out in front of you. They were so thrilled to be in New York. They were actually like a bunch of little boys. They were damn nice guys and a lot of fun to be with too."

Earl has documented that for the shoot, it's "probably from a Nikon F2 loaded with Tri-X B&W film, although the picture could be a bit deceptive and may actually be a color conversion made to look like a full-frame B&W print. Looking back, I think that we should have used more lights behind the smoke."

But alas, for the front cover, the band went with a colour-tinted outtake from the *Powerage* shoot. Of note, that's kind of what happened with *Powerage* as well. We have an untouched photo of the band on the back, with a treated image from the same shoot, just of Angus, used on the front.

"Yes," continues Earl, back to *Highway to Hell*, "and the horns were painted onto the picture later; they weren't there when we shot the picture. I didn't think the tail thing was done very well. Because this picture was taken from the earlier album, they had to improve it for this album (laughs). So they did an airbrush job on it. Like I say, the horns are okay, but I think the tail looks ridiculous, very odd. For that shoot, which was in our studio, they were there for one to two hours. That's done with studio lights using a light gray paper background. There's one light, in an umbrella held high above them."

Earl writes that Houghton used "Ektachrome film within a Hasselblad 500EL camera equipped with an 80mm Planar lens, using a single Balcar studio strobe, umbrella reflector and a Calumet generator."

As for the live album, says Earl, "Obviously the guitar is broken off and there's some ketchup there. But that's a studio shot as well; we never did live performance. It's something that we absolutely refused to do. Plus the lighting's too good to be a live shot."

Steinbicker and Houghton also worked together on Cheap Trick, Ted Nugent, The Boyzz, Ram Jam, and Derringer, to name the harder-rocking acts, i.e. bands in AC/DC's wheelhouse. But the glory days were soon over.

"Yes, when the record companies got sold, the big art directors lost their jobs," explains Earl. "We broke up at the end of '79. I helped Jim out several times after that, but then he just up and left and nobody knows where he went to. His sister, just about two years ago, contacted me and they were looking for him. The photography business was falling apart by the end of the '70s. Payment rates were going way down. There were too many photographers. Clients used to pay $1,000, but now everybody could do everything for $500. And it wasn't just records; this was across the photography business. In fact, there was a mass meeting in '79 of all the photographers in New York, and they tried to figure out a way of setting prices but we couldn't agree on anything (laughs). Both myself and Jim walked out of the meeting and we were done."

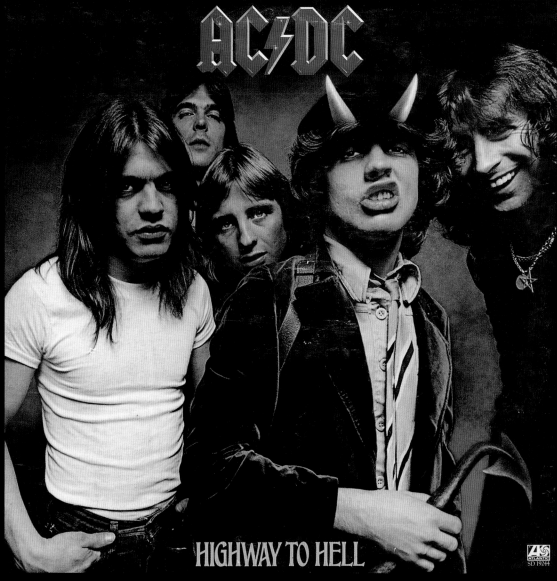

14
LET THERE BE ROCK:

**FIRST LIVE ALBUM,
IF YOU WANT BLOOD
YOU'VE GOT IT**

Supplanting a proposed greatest hits pack called *12 of the Best, If You Want Blood You've Got It*, issued October 13, 1978, was designed for the same purpose: to focus fans' ears and eyes on a few key anthems in hopes of a first hit in America, with the bonus being the added energy of a live rendition. That is this band's forte, not because AC/DC live are better than other great bands but because simpler songs—simple in construction as well as lack of studio window dressing—benefit comparatively in a run-down theater versus the likes of "Bohemian Rhapsody" (to be extreme about it).

AC/DC do not disappoint in the task either, playing tightly wound and on a mission, incorporating crowd participation, and allowing Bon to relax about what's going on behind him and lead the proceedings with charm and confidence, especially during "The Jack," which nearly devolves into a jam. Extending the crowd participation notion, producers Harry Vanda and George make sure we get to hear lots of handclapping and hollering, making *If You Want Blood* a live album of the period, famously akin to standard-bearers *Alive!* and *Alive II* from Kiss, issued in 1975 and 1977, respectively.

Ensuring a festive atmosphere is the fact that this was a very loud show at the Apollo Theatre in Glasgow, April 30, 1978, with Scotland being the ancestral home base for Malcolm and Angus as well as Bon. Underscoring the point, the band's "Rocker" encore was preceded by a minute of the band's old "Fling Thing" B-side, which is actually an instrumental segment of the Scottish traditional tune "Loch Lomond" (this was not included on the album). For the occasion, the band came out kitted in the blue-and-white jersey of the Scottish national football team, which had just qualified for the World Cup.

Before "Rocker," it's just future classic rock classic after future classic rock classic (!), basically a flawless greatest hits-type set of ten songs on, at the time, one piece of uncommonly long vinyl at fifty-two minutes, hence the record's reputation as sounding compromised. Nor did the single-LP format help with respect to impact. After all, this was the age of the double-LP gatefold live album, sometimes with extra goodies. To be sure there are classic singles, like *Live at Leeds* (The Who), *Foghat Live*, *Go for What You Know* (Pat Travers Band), and *Unleashed in the East* (Judas Priest). But the accolades were reserved for the Humble Pie and Allman Brothers Fillmore doubles, plus *Made in Japan* (Deep Purple), *All the World's a Stage* (Rush), *Frampton Comes Alive!* (Peter Frampton), *Double Live Gonzo!* (Ted Nugent), *Live and Dangerous* (Thin Lizzy), *Strangers in the Night* (UFO), and the aforementioned Kiss spreads. I'm just talking from experience—*If You Want Blood* got forgotten by my friends and me fast, especially when *Highway to Hell* and *Back in Black* arrived. Bottom line: Fans thought less of you if your live album was a single.

Was this a good album cover? To be sure, Angus impaled by a guitar is a great idea (courtesy of Atlantic art director Bob Defrin). But the shot by Jim Houghton, taken pre-show at Paradise Theater in Boston, is blurry, and the colors are dull. Arguably the back cover features a better shot, and subtly—or subconsciously—the idea of going back to the band logo from two records earlier seemed somehow "defeatist."

And if I may go on further, compounded by the tapered sound of the original vinyl, my headbanging buds and I were perfectly happy with the original studio versions of these songs from *Powerage* and *Let There Be Rock*, if slightly less so for the earlier material. Really, it was only

"Rocker" that stood out as substantially juiced to the point of making the original obsolete.

On a finer academic point, along with "Fling Thing," "Dog Eat Dog" and "Down Payment Blues" were performed at the Glasgow show but not included on the album. There was also a bit of soloing from "Rocker" excluded, as the label strived, again ill-advised, to keep the album at a single piece of vinyl. "Gimme a Bullet" was performed at sound check but not at the show later that night.

Back to the positive, *If You Want Blood You've Got It* beat *Powerage* to gold status, getting certified as such on October 14, 1980, along with *Let There Be Rock*, following upon the band's first certification ever, a gold award for *Highway to Hell*. Helping it toward a level of iconic status is the fact that forty years hence, it remains the only Bon Scott-era AC/DC live album ever issued. Perhaps a reassessment of the album's single-LP status is in order as well. For starters, there's something punk rock about the idea of getting in and getting out, reinforced by the cover art. Second, we might view the album as a metaphor for the brevity of Bon's time with us. Couple this with the fact that we never got a later-arriving archival document and somehow, *If You Want Blood You've Got It*, however bare bones, locks in for us forever the magic of Bon Scott at his peak.

Hoping for an anthemic hit in America, 1978

Aragon Ballroom, Chicago, September 22, 1978

Bon, Mal, Angus, Phil, and the new guy, Cliff, at New York's Palladium, August 24, 1978.

15
RISING POWER:

THE MUTT LANGE-PRODUCED *HIGHWAY TO HELL*

There'd been too much work done, too much reputation gained, and too much ambition for AC/DC not to expect more. Australian and European success for AC/DC hadn't translated yet in the United States, but the band couldn't be abandoned. What they needed was fresh production, said the brass; and George and Vanda, who'd done every record so far, were told to sit this one out. The band was incensed but relented. Eddie Kramer was called, but his abrasive personality rubbed this insular, ambitious, and bull-headed bunch of oddballs the wrong way and things quickly devolved. Sessions in Miami broke down, with things coming to a head when Eddie suggested the band cover Spencer Davis Group. Kramer, a South African by birth, was fired and replaced by Robert John "Mutt" Lange, another southern African (born in what is present-day Zambia); and the band was forced to find a new gear, very much the way Joe Elliott from Def Leppard once framed it for me, having run headlong into Mutt when it came time for their second album, *High 'n' Dry*.

Also like Def Leppard, the guys in AC/DC found themselves recording—and for a long time, three months—in the United Kingdom, essentially their new business address anyway. Sessions toward what would become the immense *Highway to Hell* album, issued July 27, 1979, would take place at The Roundhouse in London; and by all accounts, this new precocious producer had a few tricks up his sleeve. Having worked with The Motors, City Boy, and most notably The Boomtown Rats (on two excellent-sounding records that are vastly different from each other), Mutt was a trained singer and indeed trained Bon, teaching him how to manage his breathing and also joining in on background vocals, although keeping himself distant

This spread: Angus perfects his spin at the Palladium in New York, June 9, 1979.

in the mix lest he upset the essence of the band's sound. He also collaborated with Angus on guitar solos, which raised some eyebrows, and taught him how to work sitting down in the control room. As important, Mutt liked to tear apart and rebuild songs, as can be attested by the difference between the band's 1977 demo of "Touch Too Much" and its final flowering, which is, alas, a completely different song, sharing nothing more than a title.

There's no doubt that Atlantic wanted a more radio-friendly AC/DC. As it would turn out, radio was definitely friendlier to the band this time around and the record was a big hit. But why that is has to be chalked up to abstracts and intangibles. If anything, *Highway to Hell* in composite is even heavier than *Powerage*; and even within the realm of production, neither record is less radio-friendly than the other. What it comes down to is songs and, sure, a tiny bit of polish, a slight increase in professionalism, a few more backing vocals, plus guitar solos that sound effortless and yet have been worked hard, drawing blood. In other words, it's a bunch of little things, even if in the end the product mix is much the same, no less or more accessible on substance but just nudged over to the high rent side of town on style.

At the heavy end of *Highway to Hell* there's "Girls Got Rhythm," "Walk All Over You," "Touch Too Much," and "Beating Around the Bush," the latter featuring a riff more than a little reminiscent of Fleetwood Mac's "Oh Well." These are all weirdly placed one after another, to comprise most of side 1 of the original vinyl. Lighthearted and tuneful are "Get It Hot," "If You Want Blood (You've Got It)," and "Love Hungry Man," all in a row in the middle of side 2. (Amusingly, Angus considers "Love Hungry Man" the worst song he ever wrote.)

Closing the album is "Night Prowler," essentially a bluesy ballad, which nonetheless unfortunately took on new life as a serial-killer song when in 1985 the "Night Stalker" Richard Ramirez was discovered to be an AC/DC fan, even leaving an AC/DC ball cap at one of his crime scenes. This leaves the two biggest hits from the record, "Shot Down in Flames" and "Highway to Hell," to perform the heavy lifting, neither particularly commercial or accessible; but then again, radio and the masses at this point were buying what AC/DC were selling, no changes to the recipe necessary. Indeed, the end result was a record that had finally rendered AC/DC an "it" band, "all the rage," already (yet erroneously) considered fully successful in the eyes of a long-suffering fan base now excited that their cult heroes were showing up in their monthly supply of *Circus*, *Creem* and *Hit Parader* magazines and, in fact, treated with some level of respect in those hallowed pages.

The World Series of Rock with Aerosmith, Ted Nugent, Journey, Thin Lizzy, and the Scorpions, Cleveland Municipal Stadium, Cleveland, Ohio, July 28, 1979

With Rick Nielsen of Cheap Trick, *Rockpalast* television studios, Köln, West Germany, August 1979

16
HAVE A DRINK ON ME:
FIRST RIAA CERTIFICATION

It's a confluence of events, really, that finally converted AC/DC from a long-simmering buzz band into a modestly thriving property. Pertinently, just after *Highway to Hell* was birthed, the band signed a new management deal with powerhouse managers Steve Leber and David Krebs and their younger charge Peter Mensch, soon to become a titan in his own right (formally the company was called Contemporary Communications Corporation, or CCC, but it's commonly known as Leber Krebs). And so because of the songs, because of Mutt Lange, because of some smart moves at the business end, and because it was just AC/DC's time, *Highway to Hell* would earn the band their first gold record certified by the Recording Industry Association of America (RIAA), the album reaching that plateau on December 6, 1979, a quick four months after its appearance in the shops.

The most notable and immediate thing Leber Krebs did for the band was put them on tour in the United States playing big places in support of Ted Nugent, another Leber Krebs act, with a third from the stable, Scorpions, also newly signed, completing a powerhouse three-pronged entertainment package. Krebs also included his new charges on huge festival dates, which usually featured the fattest cats from his bullpen, Aerosmith.

As soon as *Highway to Hell* had hit the shops, in early July 1979, the band was on the road continuously, buoyed by their new situation and executing a couple of tour legs in the United States but also hitting mainland Europe, Ireland, and the United Kingdom, where on August 18 and 19, they were part of a festival package supporting The Who. Back in America again, now AC/DC were the headliners, going on after the Pat Travers Band and then back in Europe, after Def Leppard, also newly signed to Leber Krebs and, like AC/DC, more or less being managed out of the U.K. office by Mensch. Next the band was in Germany, with Judas Priest as support, when they received word that their new record had gone gold.

Of course, *Highway to Hell*'s certification story doesn't end there. The album would reach platinum on March 18, 1980, and was likely at a million copies in the United States at the time of Bon's death the previous month. Accompanying its initial certification were chart placements of #2 in France, #8 in the United Kingdom, and #17 on Billboard in the United States, with sales outside of America also garnering multiple gold and platinum awards. As usual, the happiest place was back home in Australia, where the album had now shifted in excess of 350,000 units. But most impressively, *Highway to Hell* would sell steadily throughout the 1980s, swept up by the mania surrounding *Back in Black*, to the point where it now sits at seven times platinum in the United States, putting it second behind its gravity-defying successor.

Perhaps most impressive of all, *Highway to Hell* got there on the strength of its sturdy deep tracks, producing essentially one smash single, with the band not bowing to outside pressure to change who they were and remain true to themselves to this day. To be sure, Malcolm and Angus relented on letting someone else do what George and Vanda had been doing and even took advice well. But bottom line, *Highway to Hell* is a rip-snortin' AC/DC album through and through, hard and heavy as always, and yet remains as most fans' pick for greatest AC/DC album of all time.

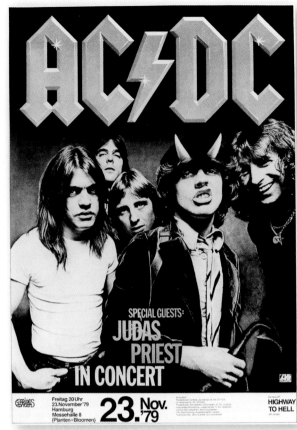

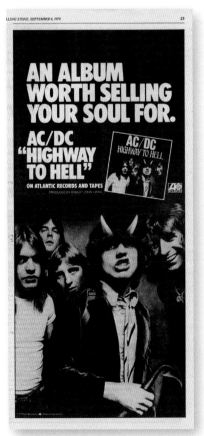

PART 2
GEORDIE

The new new guy, Brian
Johnson, De Montfort Hall,
Leicester, U.K., October 1980

17
MISS ADVENTURE:
BON SCOTT DIES

There are the facts, but there are also some questions that remain unanswered about the tragic demise of Bon Scott. The facts are this: AC/DC had returned from Australia to London in early 1980 to work on the follow-up to *Highway to Hell*. Bon's last contribution came on February 15, when he provided scratch drums as the band put together future *Back in Black* songs "Have a Drink on Me" and "Let Me Put My Love into You." Bon's last recording is considered to be a jam session with French band Trust on a rendition of AC/DC's "Ride On" quite properly recorded at Scorpio Sound two days earlier.

When not working, Bon was out hell-raising, notably hanging out with Pete Way and Paul "Tonka" Chapman from UFO, both heroin users at the time and both now sadly passed. The other fact is this: After a night of heavy partying that included a visit to a club called The Music Machine, in the early morning hours of February 19, Bon died in the tiny Renault 5 of his friend Alistair Kinnear. In a statement made the next day to authorities, Kinnear said that arriving at Bon's apartment in Victoria for a drop-off, Bon had passed out and couldn't be roused—this was about 3 a.m. He had told the *Evening Standard* that as he picked Bon up to begin their night, he was already drunk; and when they got to the club, "he was drinking four whiskies straight in a glass at a time."

Kinnear then drove to his own place at 67 Overhill Road in East Dulwich, parked his car out front, covered Bon in a blanket, and went inside. Emerging at 7:45 p.m. on the 19th after sleeping all day, Kinnear went to check on Bon and found him curled around the gearshift with his neck in an awkward position and his dental plate dislodged. Bon was rushed to King's College Hospital and declared dead by way of acute alcohol poisoning and "death by misadventure" (hypothermia is part of the legend as well, but it's not in the official documents). The coroner added that specifically death was due to pulmonary respiration of vomit—choking on vomit. After his dutiful report to authorities and his comments to the press, Kinnear, rumored to be a music journalist, was never seen again. In addition, Bon's apartment, a shared space, was promptly ransacked, with his TV and video machine and other belongings getting stolen.

The key question is whether heroin was involved. Bon had been surrounded by friends and girlfriends and minders who seemed skilled at buying and selling heroin, not to mention rock star buddies like the guys in UFO who were openly using. Some are adamant that Bon had tried it, might have been doing it, might not have been, or that he might have been a novice who had an accident. Arguably more heartbreaking is Paul Chapman's musing that on the night, Bon might have taken off to get some heroin to bring back to Paul and others who were using in hopes of keeping the party going, which, Tonka says, was always Bon's main concern. For his part, Chapman says after losing track of him that crazy night, he never saw him again.

The other mystery has to do with what time of day on the 19th Bon was discovered unresponsive. Chapman talks about phone calls between him and Joe Bloe or Joe King and Bon's dealing girlfriend Silver Smith that place the discovery earlier in the day—in fact, in the morning. Then comes the exchange of numbers with respect to informing Malcolm. But it's really neither here nor there. Myself having known Tonka personally as well as Pete Way for that matter (he's also tied up in this), it's very possible Paul was confusing the 19th for the 20th.

AC/DC briefly considered ending the band, but instead, they quickly found Brian Johnson and had *Back in Black* finished and in the shops inside of six months following Bon's death. The album—and more notably its front cover—proved to be a bigger and more lasting tribute than any fancy funeral could ever match.

Bon Scott performs at Long Beach Arena, Long Beach, California, September 10, 1979.

Bon Scott's death certificate, February 19, 1980, from the General Register Office

18

SEND FOR THE MAN:

MALCOLM OFFERS BRIAN JOHNSON A JOB

At the funeral for Bon Scott back in Australia, Bon's dad, Chick, implored the boys to carry on, adding that Bon would have wanted it that way. AC/DC also had already more than tucked into what was to become *Back in Black* when Bon died, and Mal and Angus were pumped about the new songs.

As a result, and as they intimated in the press, it was full steam ahead for finding a vocalist quickly. Considered for the job were Terry Slesser from Back Street Crawler and Buzz Shearman from Moxy—AC/DC had supported both bands live back at the beginning, which served well enough as auditions. Then there was Noddy Holder from Slade; he makes some sense, as did Gary Holton from Heavy Metal Kids. Scotland-born Allan Fryer from Aussie rockers Fat Lip was considered, with Fryer soon winding up in AC/DC-alikes Heaven with Mark Evans. Stevie Wright from The Easybeats was also mentioned. In addition, the Australian Jimmy Barnes from Cold Chisel had been rumored to be considered, although Barnes says he was never contacted.

Bon Scott's old band Fraternity (now called Fang) had supported Geordie in the United Kingdom back in the early 1970s, and he had been impressed with Brian Johnson, the band's lead singer, likening him to Little Richard. He particularly loved it when Johnson collapsed to the floor and kept wailing away, not knowing that in

Brian at his North Shields home, October 14, 1980

Brian Johnson (far right) with Geordie

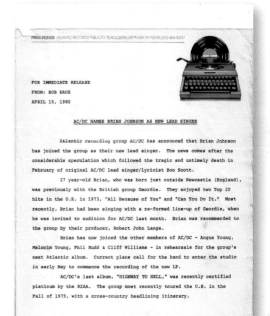

PRESS RELEASE ATLANTIC RECORDS PUBLICITY 75 ROCKEFELLER PLAZA, NY 10019 (212) 484-8200

FOR IMMEDIATE RELEASE
FROM: BOB KAUS
APRIL 15, 1980

AC/DC NAMES BRIAN JOHNSON AS NEW LEAD SINGER

        Atlantic recording group AC/DC has announced that Brian Johnson
has joined the group as their new lead singer. The news comes after the
considerable speculation which followed the tragic and untimely death in
February of original AC/DC lead singer/lyricist Bon Scott.

        27 year-old Brian, who was born just outside Newcastle (England),
was previously with the British group Geordie. They enjoyed two Top 20
hits in the U.K. in 1973, "All Because of You" and "Can You Do It." Most
recently, Brian had been singing with a re-formed line-up of Geordie, when
he was invited to audition for AC/DC last month. Brian was recommended to
the group by their producer, Robert John Lange.

        Brian has now joined the other members of AC/DC - Angus Young,
Malcolm Young, Phil Rudd & Cliff Williams - in rehearsals for the group's
next Atlantic album. Current plans call for the band to enter the studio
in early May to commence the recording of the new LP.

        AC/DC's last album, "HIGHWAY TO HELL," was recently certified
platinum by the RIAA. The group most recently toured the U.S. in the
Fall of 1979, with a cross-country headlining itinerary.

A page from the legendary *Rock`n` Roll Comics* recounts Brian's entry to the ranks.

fact that Johnson had been struck with an appendicitis attack. Bon had also nicked from Brian the idea of carrying around Angus on his shoulders, having seen Brian do that with Geordie's Vic Malcolm.

In any event, Angus and Mal remembered Bon telling them about Brian; and Mutt Lange had heard of him, too. A fan from Chicago had also mailed a tape of a Geordie album to the CCC offices in New York. By 1979, Brian had seen his career with Geordie peter out; and he had been separated from his wife and living at home, running a small auto parts company. He tells the story of getting a call from the German receptionist in the U.K. office of Leber Krebs and initially turning down the offer of an audition, saying he was too old and he couldn't afford the trip to London. Then Brian got a call from a buddy offering 350 British pounds to come sing an advertising jingle for the Hoover vacuum company—in London. He called back Peter Mensch's office and said, "Sure, I'll come in."

Once in London, wires got crossed and he found himself shooting pool with AC/DC's roadies downstairs while Mal and Angus were upstairs waiting for him, now an hour late. "At least he plays pool," was the hopeful sign. Once down to business, Brian sang "Whole Lotta Rosie" and Ike and Tina Turner's "Nutbush City Limits" with the guys, lubricated by a Newcastle Brown Ale offered to him by Mal. There was a second trip and a subsequent return to Newcastle.

Back up north, Brian had bought a bottle of whiskey for his dad's birthday and was waiting for his parents to get home when the phone rang. It's Mal, but Brian thought it was a hoax and made him call back ten minutes later, which he did. Brian was offered the job and was told that they'd be recording the album in the Bahamas. Brian said he was good to go, hung up, and cracked dad's bottle of whiskey for a lonely toast to himself. Brian Johnson became AC/DC's new singer on March 29, 1980, with the official announcement coming on April 15. The press release said that he was 27 years old, but he was in fact 32, the same age Bon Scott was when he made *Highway to Hell.*

19

BACK IN BUSINESS

AC/DC ISSUE

BACK IN BLACK

When Brian Johnson told his kid brother he'd gotten the AC/DC gig, he was not to be believed . . . because the conversation took place on April 1. But it was true, of course, with "Jonna" soon off to E'Zee Hire Studios in North London for rehearsals in advance of the band's trip to Compass Point in the Bahamas to begin work proper. London had been preferred but nothing was available. Polar Studios in Stockholm, recently generating Led Zeppelin's *In Through the Out Door*, was also considered, but it was also booked. In the end, jetting off to the Bahamas came with certain tax advantages, plus who wouldn't jump at the chance, especially given recent traumas?

The facilities were spartan, with the guys living in concrete blocks lorded over by a female caretaker who gave the guys spears to guard their living quarters against theft. Over at the studio, the room sound was dry, with Angus compensating with a wireless system. Capable producing genius Mutt Lange and his equally adept engineer, Tony Platt, helped make sure the new record would sound large and analog, with *Back in Black* winding up richer and groovier even than *Highway to Hell*.

Fortunately, the songs were more or less banged together before the band left England, resulting in a mere six weeks to get the job done. At the lyric end, the guys decided to put aside anything Bon had come up with, lest they be accused of profiting off his death. (Tour manager

Ian Jeffery talked about a folder featuring fully fifteen sets of lyrics.) Brian was asked to give it a go and he did, with the credits for every song reading "Young, Young and Johnson." Anything compromised at Compass Point, given limited equipment and the slow arrival of the band's own gear (Iron Maiden would complain about the place as well), was fixed in the mix, which took place at Electric Lady Studios in New York.

Issued July 25, 1980, *Back in Black* has been massaged into the very fiber of pop culture consciousness to the point where its songs pulse through the DNA of even the most casual music fans. "You Shook Me All Night Long," "Hells Bells," and the classic anthem-of-all-anthems title track are the flagship hits that everybody of a certain vintage knows, the latter rife with pregnant pauses and punctuated by stomping rhythms. The rest of the album—seven more raucous rockers—comprise a batch of tracks that sit between the southern rock vibe of *Powerage* and the dependable stacked pancakes of chords we hear on *Highway to Hell*, all with a shocking new voice up top, one that is more extreme than Bon's and equal of swagger.

But one thing about *Back in Black* has always been a source of cognitive dissonance. Heavy as the record is (certainly for 1980, and certainly for such a mainstream success), *Back in Black*

Orpheum Theater, Boston, Massachusetts, October 9, 1980

Brian, from a three-night stand at the Hammersmith Odeon, London, November 1980

This spread and following: Toledo Speedway Jam II, Toledo, Ohio, Augst 17, 1980. This was the last time AC/DC would raise the curtain on another act until 2003.

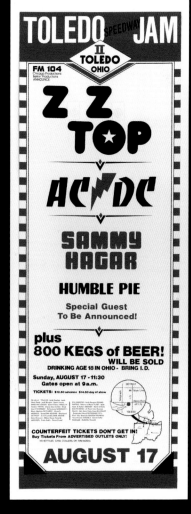

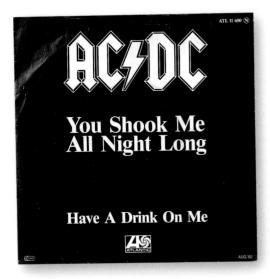

AC/DC

You Shook Me All Night Long

Have A Drink On Me

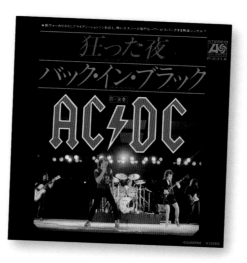

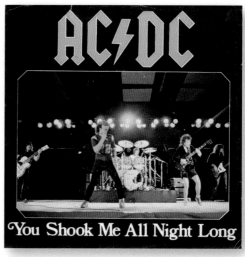

You Shook Me All Night Long

HELL'S BELLS

WHAT DO YOU DO FOR MONEY HONEY

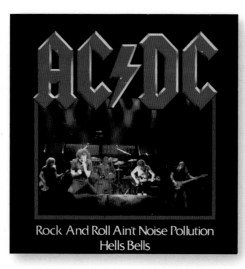

Rock And Roll Ain't Noise Pollution
Hells Bells

HELLS BELLS

is much more celebratory than would be suggested by its somber cover art (and title). In fact, the band wanted to make the sleeve completely black, to represent their sincere mourning for the loss of Bon. But they relented to label requests to frame the iconic AC/DC logo in a light gray. As well, with the original vinyl issue, the titling was embossed. To be sure, the end result is tasteful, but again, if you dispense with the strong visuals, *Back in Black* sounds like a very happy and happening party, one led by a toastmaster that sounds like he's been part of the gang all along, an old soul in love with his hard-rocking brothers and the boozing life he's now about to lead. Tens of millions agreed: forty-plus years on, *Back in Black* sits at an estimated 50 million copies sold worldwide—and never an unkind word sent its wondrous way.

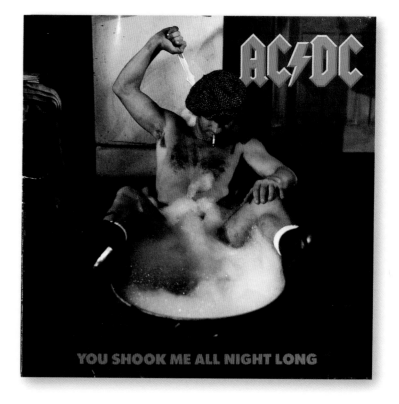

YOU SHOOK ME ALL NIGHT LONG

20
ALL SCREWED UP:
ATLANTIC ISSUES *DIRTY DEEDS* IN NORTH AMERICA

At the Palau Municipal d`Esports, Barcelona, Spain, January 15, 1981

Atlantic in the United States had famously rejected AC/DC's third album, *Dirty Deeds Done Dirt Cheap*, back in 1976, ticking off the band and their then manager Michael Browning, as well as Phil Carson, who had signed the band to the label out of the U.K. office. Flash forward four years, immediately following the death of Bon Scott, the New York office suddenly had a change of heart and was itching to put out the album. This was against the band's wishes, although David Krebs, AC/DC's manager at the time (albeit at arm's length, with Peter Mensch handling the day-to-day) has told me that he doesn't even remember there being a dispute and opines that if it had been a big deal, surely he could have stopped it.

But Carson has also explained to me in no uncertain terms that the band was dead-set against it, relenting only when demands that a clarifying sticker be placed on the album were met, with the eventual release taking place on March 27, 1981. Carson told me that *Back in Black* had sold in the region of five million copies by this point. That sounds a little high, but three million worldwide wouldn't be out of order. In any event, he also says that he threatened to quit over the decision—pinned on new Atlantic President Doug Morris, who had just replaced Jerry Greenberg—and wishes he had, because the band wanted to get him more involved in perhaps managing them, given that they were on the outs with Peter Mensch and CCC.

There were at least a couple of arguments against issuing *Dirty Deeds* at this point. First, their fans would see the band as trying to cash in on Bon's death. Second, with new and potential new fans, the record would cause confusion as to which was the new album, *Back in Black* or *Dirty Deeds*. You can throw *For Those About to Rock* into the mix as well, because that was going to hit the shops in eight months' time. Compounding the distress over the matter was the fact that the band had grown by leaps and bounds through the four studio albums since *Dirty Deeds*, as well as the fact that Bon was singing the songs and not Brian. But Carson says that Morris told him that executive bonuses were on the line and putting out *Dirty Deeds* would take care of that pretty easily. What turmoil it would cause for the guys in the band was secondary.

Carson makes an interesting point about what proceeded to happen out in the marketplace. Just like Carson (as well as Morris) predicted, the record shifted a couple million units pretty quickly, while certifying platinum on June 3, 1981 (in other words, almost immediately). But Carson had warned Morris that the situation would set a new lower sales plateau for the band. Now, no one knows whether the fact that AC/DC never sold anywhere near *Back in Black* numbers ever again had anything to do with a 1981 issue of *Dirty Deeds*, but in fact Carson's prediction to Morris came true. *For Those About to Rock* marked a deep decline, currently sitting at four times platinum, and the band never saw diamond, let alone double diamond, ever again.

All of this might have been a tempest in a teapot and lacking in correlation, but like I say, we'll never know. Then again, *Dirty Deeds Done Dirty Cheap* is now officially the band's second-greatest-selling album of all time, at six times platinum. In other words, not only did Angus and Malcolm notch for themselves a huge hit record—out of thin air, out of nothing—but they also got to see their creative work from that period now properly distributed to millions more fans, along with the validation, in those sorts of numbers, that the album wasn't so bad after all.

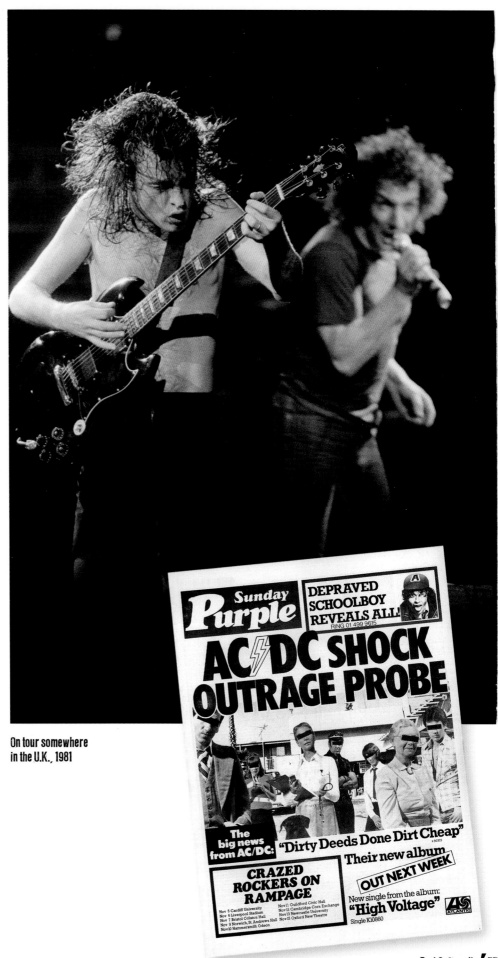

On tour somewhere
in the U.K., 1981

21

STAND UP:

HEADLINING THE SECOND ANNUAL MONSTERS OF ROCK

Donington Park, U.K., August 22, 1981.

Headling the second-ever Monsters of Rock at Castle Donington Raceway turned out to be an AC/DC career highlight on paper only. Wind, rain, and mud conspired to put a dampener on the event start to finish, although some degree of mercy was spared upon our heroes.

Opening the show that blustery August 22, 1981, NWOBHM act More, followed by tough American southern rockers Blackfoot. Slade did well to keep the crowd cheery, surely also amusing Brian Johnson, whose old band Geordie always played second fiddle in the early '70s to Noddy Holder and his foot-stomping charges. Blue Öyster Cult were next and plagued by horrible sound. The pelting rain got into the band's keyboards, and an aborted BBC filming of the event caused surge issues with the PA systems. Whitesnake were apparently firing on all cylinders, arguably stealing the show from the headliners.

Once the headliners hit the stage, the doomed vibe of Donington '81 unfortunately continued. This was only AC/DC's third outdoor show ever in the U.K. and conditions obviously weren't ideal. For props, all they had was their iconic "Hells Bells" bell—and the lack of visuals was not made up for by good audio. As road manager Ian Jeffrey explained, the BBC had managed to blow out the bottom end from the PA, to the point where AC/DC were forced to struggle through bass-less (Jeffrey likened it to the sound of "a comb with a little bit of toilet paper on it"). Compounding matters, the eight months of celebration in support of *Back in Black* was now fully six months in the rear-view mirror, given that AC/DC hadn't played live since February 28 back in Melbourne.

Nor did that mean that the guys were well rested. They were, in fact, neck-deep in the difficult birthing, across the channel in Paris, of *For Those About to Rock*, and probably at this point a little bit worried that they weren't living up to the standard set by the meteoric present record. What's more, the band and their accountant and lawyer were squeezing Leber Krebs for a reduction in management commission from fifteen percent down to five percent, and David Krebs wasn't budging. Despite Krebs flying to Paris repeatedly to get the band reupped, relations were deteriorating and the band was realizing a change of management was imminent—as would be a change of producer, which had likely crossed their minds more than a few times during the making of the new album.

As a result of these distractions, the Donington set list consisted of five songs from *Back in Black* and ten earlier crowd favorites, disappointing the diehards who might have been looking to hear a work in progress or two.

The disappointment at Donington wouldn't weigh on the guys forever. There were milestone gigs before it and there'd be milestone gigs to come, including two redemptive performances at Donington in 1991 and 1984, the latter of which is considered by many to be the greatest Monsters of Rock of all time.

22

FIRE YOUR GUNS:

THE EIGHTH ALBUM, FOR THOSE ABOUT TO ROCK

Whether it was because AC/DC were no longer hungry or because of the pressure to at least equal *Back in Black*, *For Those About to Rock* was a grind in the making and was then received with mixed feelings, Malcolm famously reflected immediately after that he wasn't sure whether they'd hit the marks as they hit the road and shot those cannons off every night.

The problems began with the choice of studio. Set up in France, sessions at Pathé-Marconi were aborted after two weeks, with the band opting to record with the Mobile One remote in an old warehouse on the outskirts of Paris, after second choice, Studio Ramses, was found to be unavailable. Vocals would have to be taken care of at Family Sound and further overdubs at H.I.S. Complicating matters, the guys weren't happy with their apartments in town; nor, as discussed, were they happy with their management situation.

But most troubling was that the songs weren't coming together. Malcolm and Angus were struggling with the writing, while Mutt Lange, in transition to the notoriously obsessive producer he would become with Def Leppard, overworked the weak material the band had until it lost its edge, sounding big and fat to be sure but no longer "cool," particularly against the exciting young acts rising up from the NWOBHM (or for that matter, both a hot Ozzy Osbourne and a hot Black Sabbath).

And there's the rub, really. When *For Those About to Rock* hit the shops on November 23, 1981, it sounded like the work of a band suddenly insulated by corporate privilege, wrapped in a gatefold of gold (well, copper), boring blurry live shot inside, not much on the front, song titles on the back along with a confusing continuation of the album title. A further note on the live shot: The tacit message received—at least by us angry metalhead kids back in the day—was ignore the record and let's get back to the tour in support of *Back in Black*, given that the shot couldn't have been from the tour for the album in which it was poorly pasted.

And again, contrasted against the burgeoning NWOBHM scene, AC/DC suddenly sounded old and tired, just like Judas Priest did with 1981's *Point of Entry* (another wobbly follow-up to a black album from 1980), both bands bested by Iron Maiden, Motörhead, Saxon, and, yes, Lange's other thing, Def Leppard. Besides the pillowy, billowy sound of the album, the songs were, in the main, slow and slow to get going, exemplified in stark fashion by the title track, which is the one place on the otherwise tedious record that this approach worked, even if the cheap ploy of cannon fire was needed to put it over the top. The title of the track (and album) is a twist on "For those about to die, we salute you" from Roman gladiator times. As for the cannons, Malcolm got the idea from watching TV footage of the royal wedding between Prince Charles and Lady Diana happening across the channel as he sat bored in Paris waiting for Lange's next set of instructions.

Beyond the title track, "Let's Get It Up" was issued as a single, with the song exemplifying the easy drinking accessibility of the album. Commercial, simple, and juvenile, the song established the chortling narrative continued through the likes of "Put the Finger on You" and "Inject the Venom," while AC/DC convinced no one of occult bona fides despite "Evil Walks" and "C.O.D.," which stood, clumsily, for "care of the devil." What's more, both of those songs are quite cheery and relaxed. And if you were struggling to stay onboard and upright, by the time you got to the first verse of "Breaking the Rules," it was for sure down for the count, the guys dialing way back on a record that hadn't turned up since the thrilling conclusion of the (too long) title track way back at the beginning of side 1. The singsongy chorus on "Night of the Long Knives" doesn't make any friends either, and then album closer "Spellbound" is one plush recline of a bluesy proposition too many.

For Those About to Rock essentially shipped platinum, receiving its official designation as such just into the new year. But it would be late 1984 when the record reached double platinum, en route to the four times platinum status it ponders as of the last certification application in 2001. That's no slouch, but nonetheless, it's a stinging disappointment given *Back in Black*'s current perch at twenty-five times platinum—and still killin' it at streaming, at a factor twenty times greater than its denigrated successor, representing the narrative that forty years after the fact, we're still stuck standing and shifting awkwardly at the wake for Bon Scott, unwilling to forget and move on.

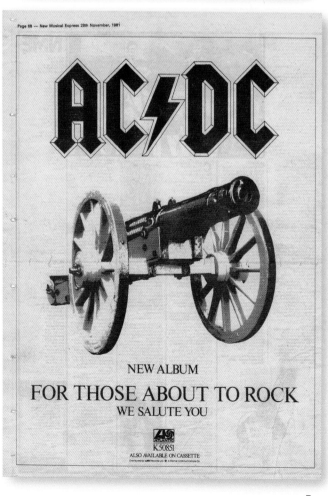

AC/DC
INJECT
THE
VENOM

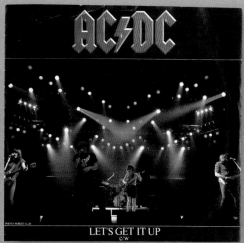

Brian and Angus work up
the Cow Palace crowd, San
Francisco, February 16, 1982.

GEORDIE - HOPE YOU LIKE IT ...

...but not enough did, so Brian was back working with his hands and not his powerful scratchpad of a voice. That was also the name of the first Geordie album, with *Hope You Like It* being issued in 1973, with every song but one written by a guitarist named Malcolm. Next came *Don't Be Fooled by the Name*, where on the front cover Brian looked like Angus. Next came 1976's *Save the World*, on which the album title was rendered in the blocky font soon to be made famous by Iron Maiden. The band's last EMI album featured a hodgepodge of players and sessions, *No Good Woman* arriving in 1978, with Brian featured on five of ten tracks.

As for the band's sound, it was easy enough for the AC/DC guys to imagine Johnson singing for them, given the rough-shod blue-collar rock of the band. Slade, Status Quo, T. Rex, and Humble Pie come to mind, but so does wobbly early AC/DC and, oddly, other Australian acts like Buffalo, Coloured Balls, and even Stevie Wright. Unlike Bon Scott's early band Fraternity, where Bon croons with sincerity, Geordie was built for pushing air, and what we hear is approximately the Brian we love, with 20 percent less vocal fry and 20 percent added versatility, given the band's tendency to mix it up, trying old-time blues, soul, and rock 'n' roll, the glam of the day and even a few songs closer to heavy metal than what AC/DC might cook up.

For those who want to cut to the chase and hear Geordie making the kind of music that might have fit at the low-charge end of the original *High Voltage*, there's some entertainment value in "Keep on Rockin'," "Give You Till Monday," "All Because of You," "Goin' Down," "So What," "Ten Feet Tall," "Francis Was a Rocker," "Fire Queen," "She's a Lady," "Mama's Gonna Take You Home," "She's a Teaser," "Going to the City," "Rock 'n' Roll Fever," and at the end of the road, *No Good Woman* bonus track "Dollars–Deutsche Marks."

Much to the annoyance of Johnson, once he became the tam-topped belter of the fastest-rising band in the land, back came a reformed Geordie. Granted, *No Sweat*, issued in 1983, featured the nucleus of the original lineup, namely Vic Malcolm on guitar, Tom Hill on bass and Brian Gibson on drums—just no Brian Johnson, because he was busy. Incidentally, even if Brian was interested in joining the boys for a blow, AC/DC's culture was famously closed shop, with Malcolm and Angus having zero tolerance for split loyalties—it would have been a non-starter.

But that didn't stop Red Bus Music from issuing in 1982 a "Brian Johnson" album called *Strange Man*, which was nothing more than a ten-track compilation of old Geordie songs. The low-level confusion over whether Brian was embarking on a solo career was compounded by the fact that the previous year, *Dirty Deeds Done Dirt Cheap* was issued with much fanfare in North America, featuring Brian's predecessor Bon Scott. That same year, MCA issued a compilation called *Brian Johnson and Geordie*, featuring the AC/DC singer's name in big letters and a picture of him (and him only) on the front and back. Then, as noted, in 1983 we got a serious enough brand-new Geordie album.

As the decades mounted, there'd be more than a dozen (depending on how you count) Geordie compilations, with the exploitative nature generally waning, as we settled into history and realized that this was a band with three-and-a-half proper albums recorded at proper studios with known producers and issued by a major label and thus worthy of study on its own merits—even if the assembled oeuvre speaks to a knees-up, foot-stompin' type of glam rock briefly fashionable and now long forgotten.

Geordie

appearing at the
RAINBOW THEATRE
Friday March 30th

NEW ALBUM
Hope you like it
Including their hot single "Don't Do
That", and their latest single
"All Because of You"
EMI 2008

EMC 3001

♥あのアニマルズの故郷、ニューキャッスルから躍り出た
炎のロックン・ロール・カルテット!! ♥これこそのりのりの大ヒットだあ——!

STEREO EOR-10476

君にすべてを
キープ・オン・ロッキン　歌＋演奏　ジョーディー
プロデューサー——エリス・エライアス・ロバート・ダノーヴァ

Geordie

Odeon
RECORDS

H￥500

Geordie

From the stompin' North-East, England's
biggest energy rock sensation.....Geordie, and their
first album that includes the favourites you put in
the charts–"Don't Do That" and "All Because Of You".
It's called "Hope You Like It".
You will.

Album EMC 3001 Cassette TC EMC 3001 Cartridge 8X EMC 3001

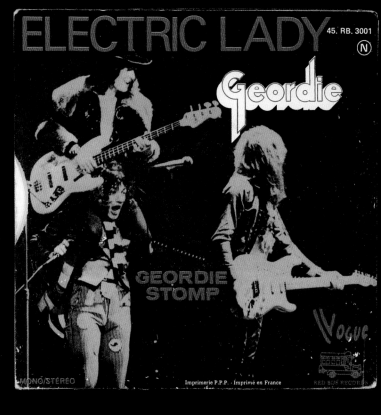

ELECTRIC LADY   45. RB. 3001   Ⓝ

Geordie

GEORDIE
STOMP

Vogue

MONO/STÉRÉO   Imprimerie P.P.P. · Imprimé en France   RED BUS RECORDS

Geordie

ELECTRIC LADY

Their New Smash Single on Emi

EMI 2048

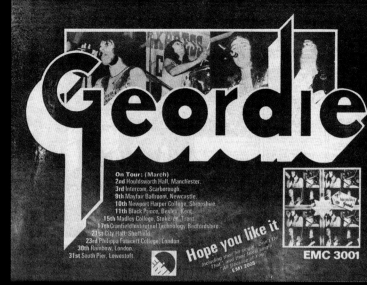

Geordie

On Tour: (March)
2nd Houldsworth Hall, Manchester.
3rd Intercom, Scarborough.
9th Mayfair Ballroom, Newcastle.
10th Newport Harper College, Shropshire.
11th Black Prince, Bexley, Kent.
15th Madley College, Stoke-on-Trent.
17th Cranfield Institute of Technology, Bedfordshire.
21st City Hall, Sheffield.
23rd Philippa Fawcett College, London.
30th Rainbow, London.
31st South Pier, Lowestoft.

Hope you like it

Including their hit single 'Don't Do That' and their latest single 'All Because of You' EMI 2008

EMC 3001

Geordie

Don't be fooled by the name

ON TOUR
April 19th Dreamland, Margate/April 22nd Quaintways, Chester
April 26th Newcastle City Hall/April 27th Barbarella's, Birmingham
April 29th Merthyr Tydfil

NEW ALBUM
EMA 764
Also available on Cassette and Cartridge

Geordie

Don't be fooled by the name

ON TOUR
April 16th Town Hall, Clacton/April 17th Lyceum, London
April 19th Dreamland, Margate/April 22nd Quaintways, Chester
April 26th Newcastle City Hall/April 27th Barbarella's, Birmingham
April 29th Merthyr Tydfil

NEW ALBUM
EMA 764
Also available on Cassette and Cartridge

FAIR DEAL

THE SOUNDS SERVICE WHICH INVESTIGATES YOUR PROBLEMS

edited by Liz Cooper

PASS THE PARCEL

ABOUT FIVE months ago, I bought a stereo unit, an EKCO ZU4L. I bought a pair of headphones which were fitted with a standard jack plug — as most headphones are — but my stereo takes a 5 pin 360 deg DIN plug. I tried all the dealers in Londonderry but couldn't get one, so I wrote to the makers of the unit, Pye of Cambridge, in September last year. Pye passed my letter to CES Services Dept., Croydon. CES passed it on to Eirco Ltd, Belfast. Eirco wrote on October 4 saying the item wasn't in stock but they would obtain one and send it to me with all possible speed.

I waited until last month, wrote to Eirco, got no reply, so wrote once again to Pye. They sent me a little card saying they had passed it to CES so I'm back where I started.

I find it hard to believe that a firm like Pye should put stereo units on the market for which accessories are virtually impossible to obtain.

I hope you can do something to help or give me advice on what I should do about. — Ken Cargill, Waterside, Londonderry.

● ALL PYE products are equipped with DIN standard sockets, a continental standard gradually being adopted in this country. Pye accessories are manufactured by Philips of which Eirco and CES are branches being the source for your query being sent to them.

I'm still at a loss to understand why they couldn't help you before but Lynne Jones, Pye's Customer Liaison Officer, is certainly willing to try now. Can you write direct to her, giving full details of your headphones etc. at PO Box 49, St. Andrew's Road, Cambridge, CB4 1DS.

AT THE beginning of August '73 I sent for a pair of brushed denim brown trousers and a matching jacket (second colour choice blue). I wanted the clothes for an occasion in September, but when the time came and I had not received my order, I went out and bought a suit. I wrote to Sujo and received my order at the end of October.

Sujo had sent a jacket and trousers, one brown and one blue — the jacket was too small, the trousers too large. I returned them saying I wasn't satisfied. In December, I received a pair of trousers in a smaller size. There was no letter attached and I no longer required them as I had bought a similar suit when my order had not arrived. I returned these with a letter.

After hearing nothing, on February 4, I wrote once more asking for a refund of my money. After two months, on April 2, I received a jacket. Once more I have returned the jacket with a letter saying I am not satisfied and would very much appreciate a refund of my money.

I would appreciate your help in ending this stupid pass-the-parcel game. — Doug Evans, Bilston, Staffs.

● When I passed your complaint to one of Sujo's directors, he was extremely upset and is now investigating the reasons behind the delay in dealing with your letters. Your refund should have arrived by the time you read this.

ABOUT a year ago I bought a stereo cassette player and radio SONY CF 620 for £150 and I have had nothing but trouble with it. Everytime I send it away to be repaired, it has to go back in again. The radio is perfect but the heads have been bad all the time. Last week I sent it away again and got it back again. The heads are now all right but now the cassettes are only playing on one speaker.

When I collected it last time I found that it had been knocked about and there is a lot of paint chipped off it. As it is really a piece of furniture it looks terrible. So I wondered if you could try to find out what they think they are playing at. I purchased the player from Lind-Air Audio, Nottingham. — David J. Cornwall, Nottingham.

● The manager of the shop concerned has arranged for your equipment to be fixed locally which means it will be ready in one week. They agree with your complaint about paint being chipped off and have replaced the part in question.

ON FEBRUARY 4 I sent away for two parts of an electronical project. The project was the P.E. Rondo complete quadrophonic Hi-Fi system. The value of the postal order I sent was £13.75. I heard nothing from them for a month and so decided to write them a letter asking for an explanation for the delay.

Now, nearly another month later, I still have not heard from them. The firm is Sonax Electronics of Edmonton, London.

Could you please find out what has happened to my order. — G. Catton, Whitley, Coventry.

● Your order was received by Sonax and you should have received their acknowledgement and parts immediately. They have no record of having received your letter.

The reason for the delay is that sending your order is that there is a hold-up on circuit boards. Mr. Ellis of Sonax assures me that your parts of the project will be with you within two weeks and he has written to you with a full explanation for the delay.

SOUNDS FAIR DEAL COUPON

Not getting a fair deal? Write to Liz Cooper, SOUNDS, Spotlight House, 1 Benwell Road, London N7 7AX. Each enquiry to Fair Deal MUST be accompanied by this coupon.

Name.......................................
Address....................................
.....................................Age.....

Disc—May 19th, 1973

From the stompin' North-East, England's
biggest energy rock sensation.....Geordie, and their
first album that includes the favourites you put in
the charts–"Don't Do That" and "All Because Of You".
It's called "Hope You Like It".
You will.

Album EMC 3001 Cassette TC EMC 3001 Cartridge 8X EMC 3001

Geordie, one of the most visually exciting bands in the country,
have returned to Britain after almost a year. Having already enjoyed
considerable chart success with a string of hit records, Geordie
now celebrate their return to these shores with the release of their
finest album to date.
"Save The World" EMC 3134

An older Geordie enjoy a tipple, September 23, 2001. They
had been rehearsing for a reunion show that took place at the
Newcastle Opera House five days later. Left to right: Derek
Rootham, Brian Johnson, Davy Whittaker, and Dave Robson.

23

BREAKING THE RULES:

THE SELF-PRODUCED *FLICK OF THE SWITCH*

Now properly huge, with three big records in a row and coming off their most lucrative and well-attended touring cycle yet, AC/DC were nonetheless still rattled by the experience of making the last album, downright paranoid about what to do next. Malcolm's response was to clean house, replacing roadies and severing ties with photographers and other associates, but most notably appointing tour manager Ian Jeffrey as the replacement for Peter Mensch and, even more notably, deciding that he'd produce the next record himself.

In addition, the band would go back to the locale of their biggest triumph, Compass Point in the Bahamas, with the idea being that they could concentrate with fewer distractions. Malcolm's drinking was getting worse, but a bigger problem was Phil Rudd, who had been smoking so much pot he was starting to hallucinate. He had also gotten a girl pregnant in France and had now hooked up with a relative of Malcolm's—after his quick and capable dispensing of his drum duties in Nassau, Phil would be ousted.

Mandate-wise, Malcolm had decided that AC/DC had to get back to rocking and rocking hard, figuring that *Back in Black* was about as produced as they should ever get. His brief to engineer Tony Platt had included the idea that he wanted the party atmosphere heard on Johnny Winter's

Backstage after a *Flick of the Switch*-era show at Joe Louis Arena, Detroit, November 17, 1983. Simon Wright is second from right.

version of Muddy Waters's classic "Mannish Boy" to pervade these sessions, also pointing to the Edgar Winter hit "Frankenstein" as inspiration.

Platt wonders whether this was achieved, remembering the sessions to me as unhappy and tense. Foremost were the problems with Phil, but there was also irritation from Angus toward Brian, whose voice wasn't in top form. In fact, Angus was no producer, and his involvement at that role was hampering Malcolm and Platt getting on with things. Brian was also saddled with doing the lion's share of the lyrics, when on the past two records the wordsmithing had been more of a collaborative effort, with Mutt Lange and even Platt pitching in. Platt also points to problems the guys had with speaker cones, the humidity of the place causing issues with audio and thus accuracy of takes. In addition, they got bored pretty fast with going to the beach, adding to the tension that culminated in Phil getting put on a plane and sent home after his parts were done but before everybody else would vacate.

Amusingly, after the album was tracked, Malcolm thought it sounded too much like *Back in Black* and Platt, with the aid of George Young back in New York, shifted the fulcrum back toward the raw and electric sound Malcolm had envisioned at the start, also adding some extra backing vocals. Of note, the official production credit would go to AC/DC, with Platt getting credit for the engineering and the mix. Platt is one of three people thanked, along with Dutch Damager and The Gorgeous Glaswegian, who are none other than Harry Vanda and George Young.

Flick of the Switch, issued August 15, 1983, was poorly received at the time, not helped in the marketplace by the label's disappointment at its prospects, with the executive branch not digging Angus's austere concept for the album cover and citing the album's lack of a clear single. "Guns for Hire" was first floated, but its wall-of-guitars sound and a scratchy Brian Johnson vocals and equally scratchy production palette conspired to limit success. "Flick of the Switch" was just too heavy, and then finally "Rising Power," with its arcane tribal beat, was just too weird—slow didn't work like it did last time (there were no cannons). The official videos for all three were done at the same time (and in one day), the theme being a quick setup surrounded by amps and flight cases, really driving home the bare-bones approach to the album, an idea that was supposed to get AC/DC back their street credibility.

It did, even if it took twenty years.

Flick of the Switch is now considered by many to be one of the great Brian Johnson-era AC/DC albums, and even for those not fully on board, it's more so considered one of the heaviest. In fact, among metalheads, it's the band's version of *Born Again* by Black Sabbath, issued the same year, both being brash, notorious, cranky, basically badass. So yes, *Flick of the Switch* essentially fulfilled Malcolm's original vision, even if that vision didn't include the record

fully stiffing in the marketplace, achieving gold status early the next year and then not finding platinum until 2001. Still, even in its day, at least as far as the heavy metal faithful were concerned, *Flick of the Switch* had AC/DC returning to its status as raucous hoodlum rockers, a band for the people, a band that could compete with any up-and-comers from the now-ending NWOBHM as well as upstarts stateside like Quiet Riot, Ratt, Mötley Crüe, Dokken, and Twisted Sister. Apropos of little, I guess, but it's my favorite of the entire Brian Johnson canon, despite no cannons.

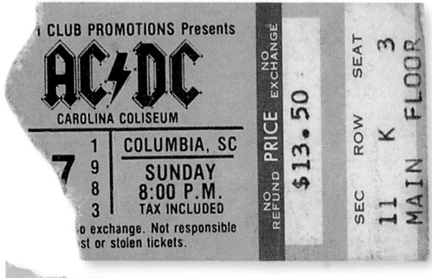

24
THIS HOUSE IS ON FIRE:

FIRST BAND TO HEADLINE MONSTERS OF ROCK TWICE

As for the band's next career highlight, that would be represented by a return to British soil as headliners of Monsters of Rock, August 18, 1984, in front of a crowd of 65,000 in good weather, with AC/DC becoming the first band to top the bill twice. The guys hadn't played the United Kingdom since October 1982 and hadn't played anywhere else for that matter since the three-month campaign in North America to close out 1983.

What's more, this was the first show in the home country for new drummer Simon Wright, who had joined in time to execute all the tour dates thus far in support of *Flick of the Switch*, as well as the music videos in support of the three singles. Wright, a 20-year-old lad from Manchester without much of a past (Tora Tora, AIIZ, Tytan), was brought on through a novel audition process in London that had each applicant first play along to a tape run by a roadie, after which if the test was passed, he'd get sent to the next round to play with the band. It's been reported that 700 drummers were looked at, with two notable players being Roxy Music's Paul Thompson and Bad Company's Simon Kirke, soon to reform his mainstay band to platinum success. In any event, it turns out that Wright was a big AC/DC fan and small in stature (like the last low-key Northerner hired), so he fit right in and got the gig. With Wright's addition, now everybody in AC/DC was U.K.-born.

Come Monsters of Rock, AC/DC were a last-minute sub when Rush had vacillated on the decision to headline and were set aside. Now AC/DC were going to have to do their thing right after Warner Bros. rivals Van Halen had left the stage, with Diamond Dave and crew riding high with "Jump," "Panama," and the rest of the *1984* album, which was rapidly outselling the last record from AC/DC.

The undercard of the bill was impressive as well, beginning with Mötley Crüe and then Accept, followed by Y&T, then Gary Moore and Ozzy Osbourne. All of them are great live acts, but then so is AC/DC, who comported themselves well enough but not exceptionally (long gaps between songs, Brian pretty regularly out of tune, reports of low energy) against the competition, augmented by the bells of *Back in Black* and the cannons of *For Those About to Rock* and closing out with a fireworks display. Then again, there were complaints about Van Halen as well, with respect to excessive guitar noodling from Eddie and David Lee Roth being Dave. This was Van Halen's first U.K. show since 1980, and it would be the last there before Sammy Hagar would become the band's new front man. By many reports, it's Ozzy Osbourne who did the best on the day, with Ozzy determined to make up for having to cancel his whole U.K. tour due to a flu bug.

AC/DC's hour-and-forty-minute set for the night, notable for its clear and powerful stage mix, was essentially a hits package; but the most recent album was represented by worthy snare-whacked opener "Guns for Hire" and then the fully headbanging "Flick of the Switch" mid-set. Half of *Back in Black* was performed (in order, "Shoot to Thrill," "Back in Black," "Rock and Roll Ain't Noise Pollution," "Hells Bells," and "Have a Drink on Me"), with the legend of *For Those About to Rock*'s title track getting a boost through its use as the night's final selection, after encore opener "T.N.T." All told, the 1984 edition is considered by many to be the best Monsters of Rock of all time, and it certainly was much more fun for AC/DC this time out, given the near disaster of 1981's storm-ravaged mudfest three years earlier.

AC/DC flight cases are lined up for inspection, Monsters of Rock, Donington Park, U.K., August 18, 1984.

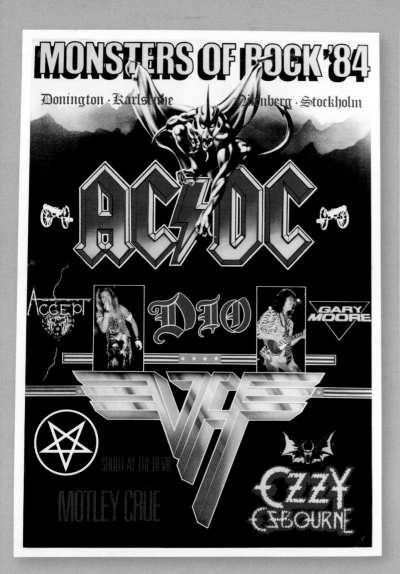

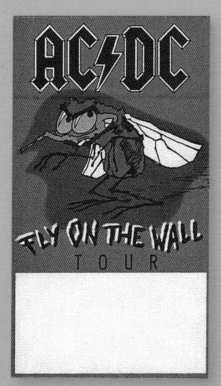

MCP & PLP FOR WOOLTARE LTD PRESENTS

MONSTERS OF ROCK

AC/DC

VAN HALEN

OZZY OSBOURNE

GARY MOORE

Y&T

ACCEPT MÖTLEY CRÜE

TOMMY VANCE

DONINGTON PARK
SATURDAY 18th AUGUST 1984

TICKETS £11.00. ADVANCE (subject to booking fee) AVAILABLE FROM:—

ABERDEEN: Other Record Shop	CARLISLE: Pink Panther	GLASGOW: Apollo Theatre Box Office	LIVERPOOL: Penny Lane Records	NOTTINGHAM: Select-a-Disc	SHEFFIELD: Cavendish Travel
AYR: Powerhouse	CHESTER: Penny Lane Records	GLOUCESTER: Leisure Centre Box Office	LIVERPOOL: T.L.C.A.	OXFORD: Apollo Theatre Box Office	SOMERSET: La Monde Travel
BANBURY: Midlands Travel	CLEETHORPES: Peter Hall Music Shop	GOOLE: Peter Hall Music Shop	LONDON: Stargreen Box Office & Albemarle	PETERBOROUGH: Wirrina Stadium Box Office	SOUTHAMPTON: Virgin Records
BARNSTAPLE: Concert Travel Club	COALVILLE: Randles	HARTLEPOOL: Other Record Shop	LONDON: National Travel	PLYMOUTH: Virgin Records	SUNDERLAND: Spinning Disk
BEWDLEY: Greyhound Records	COVENTRY: Apollo Theatre Box Office	HINDHEAD: Thames Valley & Aldershot Bus Co	LONDON: Premier B/O & Keith Prowse Limited	POOLE: Setchfields	SWANSEA: Derricks Records
BIRMINGHAM: Cyclops	DARLINGTON: Williams	HULL: Gough & Davy	MANCHESTER: Piccadilly Records	PORT TALBOT: Derricks Records	SWANSEA: South Wales Transport
BIRMINGHAM: Odeon Theatre Box Office	DERBY: Donington Park Racing Circuit	IPSWICH: Gaumont Theatre Box Office	MANSFIELD: Revolver Records	PRESTON: The Guild Hall Box Office	SWINDON: Rimes Coaches
BLACKBURN: King Georges Hall Box Office	DERBY: RE Cords	LANCASTER: Ear Ere Records	MIDDLESBOROUGH: Newhouse Music	PRESTON: Ribble Motor Services	SWINDON: Kempster & Son
BRADFORD: Bostocks	DERBY: Trent Motor Traction	LEEDS: Cavendish Travel	MILTON KEYNES: Virgin Records	READING: Listen Records	SWINDON: Cheltenham & Glos. Omnibus Co.
BRIDLINGTON: Holiday Travel	DERBY: Way Ahead	LEEDS: Barkers	NEWCASTLE-UPON-TYNE: Mike Lloyd Music	READING: Smiths Coaches	UPPER HEYFORD: Midlands Travel
BRIGHTON: Subway	DONCASTER: Ashley Adams	LEICESTER: De Montfort Hall Box Office	NEWCASTLE-UNDER-TYNE: City Hall Box Office	REIGATE: London County Greenline	WAKEFIELD: Record Bar
BRISTOL: Virgin Records	DUDLEY, W. Midlands: Concert Security Services	LEICESTER: Midland Fox	NORTHAMPTON: United Counties Bus Station	RUGBY: Midland Red South	WOLVERHAMPTON: Goulds
BURTON-ON-TRENT: RE Cords	DUNDEE: Total Entertainments	LINCOLN: The Box Office	NORWICH: HMV Records	SEVENOAKS: Furkings Box Office	WREXHAM: Phase One Records
CARDIFF: Spillers	EDINBURGH: Playhouse Theatre Box Office	LINCOLN: Lincolnshire Road Car Co.	NOTTINGHAM: Way Ahead	SHEFFIELD: Virgin Records	YORK: Sound Effects

Tickets are also available by post from: Wooltare Ltd. PO Box 123, Walsall. WS1 1TJ. Enclose Postal Orders or Cheques made payable to Wooltare Limited and S.A.E.   Tickets are £11.00 advance £12.00 on the day (People sending cheques should allow 21 days for clearance)

25 GO DOWN:

HEADLINING ROCK IN RIO

Following the band's stand at Monsters of Rock at Donington, another thirteen Monsters-type shows were played across Europe. Then it was time for another live milestone for the band, namely two nights headlining the inaugural Rock in Rio, in Rio de Janeiro, Brazil. This was a monumental affair, spanning ten nights in Brazil, playing to a total of 1.4 million people. The headliners for the event, beginning on January 11 in order through January 20, consisted of Queen, George Benson, Rod Stewart, James Taylor, AC/DC, Rod Stewart, Yes, Queen, AC/DC, and then Yes again on the last night.

On January 15, AC/DC played after Scorpions and some local acts to a crowd of 50,000; and on the 19th, they headlined above Scorpions, Ozzy Osbourne, Whitesnake, and local act Baby Consuelo e Pepeu Gomes, playing to a quarter million people. Both shows opened with Angus gleefully hacking his way through a lengthy guitar solo sequence punctuated with the call-and-response stabs from "Guns for Hire." Once it was time for that arse-kicking *Flick of the Switch* opening selection, Angus jumped off his amp and proceeded to Chuck Berry duck-walk across the stage like the loveable maniac that he is.

This spread: The band performs as part of Rock in Rio, January 1985.

The crowd went wild and were with the guys 'til the end as they played a set similar to that of the preceding tour, most notably with "Shot Down in Flames" cycled in for the departing "Flick of the Switch." The band was on fire for both performances, playing some of the selections noticeably fast, with "Let There Be Rock" particularly manic. Only "Guns for Hire" was played from *Flick of the Switch* and only "For Those About to Rock (We Salute You)" was played from the preceding record, although like Donington, this was the epic closing selection, complete with firing cannons. The show on the 15th included two additional numbers over the 19th, namely "The Jack" and rarity "Jailbreak," which was performed for the first time since 1977. Brian's vocals were better on the 19th over the 15th, with both performances noticeably a cut above his challenged time at Donington. Amusingly, Brian did both shows without his hat on

toward the end, exposing his unruly not-long, not-short mop of hair, while Angus's hair was uncommonly long at the time.

Rock in Rio '85 will reign legendary forever (granted, most famously for Queen's performance there, filmed properly and widely shown), but in reality the event was plagued with corruption and lost tons of money, with the purpose-built "Rockdome" venue, which was erected at a cost of $11.5 million, demolished shortly after the festival. Rock in Rio wouldn't be back again until 1991, and AC/DC would take a long break as well, Malcolm citing fears of overexposure, with the band not returning to touring duties until a full eight months later in support of a little something called *Fly on the Wall*.

Flexing on Rio de Janeiro's famed Ipanema Beach

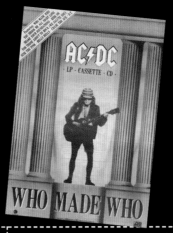

1985
AC/DC headline Rock in Rio.

January 15 and 19

1985
AC/DC issue *Fly on the Wall*.

June 28

1986
Who Made Who, part soundtrack album, part compilation.

May 24

1988
Vanda and Young are back, producing *Blow Up Your Video*.

January 18

1992
AC/DC issue the first live album of the Brian Johnson era.

October 27

1995
AC/DC's 13th album, *Ballbreaker*.

September 26

1997
In honor of Bon Scott, AC/DC issue their first box set.

November 18

2000
Brian Johnson keeps a stiff upper lip.

February 28

2009
AC/DC issue *Backtracks*, a second box set of rarities.

November 10

2012
Live at River Plate captures the band on stage in Argentina.

November 19

2014
Malcolm Young steps down.

April 16

2014
"In rock we trust, it's rock or bust."

November 28

1975
T.N.T., AC/DC`s second album.

December 1

1976
AC/DC play the Red Cow in London, their first show outside of Australia.

April 23

1976
Atlantic issues AC/DC`s international debut album, calling it *High Voltage.*

April 30

1976
AC/DC`s third Australian-only album, *Dirty Deeds Done Dirt Cheap.*

September 20

1978
AC/DC issue *Powerage,* their fifth album.

May 5

1978
*If You Want Blood You`ve Got It—* AC/DC`s first live album.

October 13

1979
AC/DC`s breakout album, the Mutt Lange – produced *Highway to Hell.*

July 27

1979
AC/DC get their first gold record in America.

December 6

1981
The second annual Monsters of Rock is headlined by AC/DC.

August 22

1981
AC/DC issue *For Those About to Rock,* a third Mutt Lange – produced album.

November 23

1983
AC/DC issue *Flick of the Switch,* self-producing for the first time.

August 15

1984
AC/DC headline Monsters of Rock for a second time.

August 18

1973
AC/DC play their first gig.

January 31

1974
The first single, "Can I Sit Next to You, Girl."

July 22

1974
Bon Scott joins AC/DC.

October 24

1975
AC/DC issue their debut album, *High Voltage*.

February 11

1977
AC/DC issue *Let There Be Rock*, their fourth album.

March 21

1977
Cliff Williams is hired as AC/DC`s new bassist.

May 27

1977
AC/DC play Austin, Texas, their first show in America.

July 27

1977
AC/DC wins over a tough New York crowd, playing CBGB.

August 24

1980
The death of Bon Scott.

February 19

1980
Brian Johnson becomes AC/DC`s new singer.

March 29

1980
AC/DC usher in the 1980s with *Back in Black*.

July 25

1981
Atlantic issues *Dirty Deeds Done Dirt Cheap*—five years late.

March 27

1988
Malcolm bows out of a tour to take care of his alcoholism.

May 3–November 13

1990
The Razors Edge represents a big comeback for AC/DC.

September 21

1990
Back in Black certifies ten times platinum in the United States.

October 23

1991
AC/DC conquer Russia.

September 28

2000
AC/DC appear on *Saturday Night Live*.

March 18

2003
AC/DC begin a year featuring shows with The Rolling Stones.

February 18

2003
AC/DC enter the Rock and Roll Hall of Fame.

March 10

2003
AC/DC rock Toronto on a grand scale.

July 30

2008
AC/DC deliver the long-awaited *Black Ice* album.

October 20

2015
AC/DC perform at the 57th Grammy Awards.

February 8

2016
The last AC/DC show to date with Brian.

February 28

2016
Axl Rose fronts AC/DC.

May 7–September 20

2017
Rest in peace, George Young and Malcolm Young.

October 22 and November 18

2020
Power Up.

November 13

26
SHAKE YOUR FOUNDATIONS:
AC/DC ISSUE *FLY ON THE WALL*

All the Monsters of Rock and Rock in Rio triumphs couldn't paper over the facts 'n' cracks that AC/DC had slipped in both sales and critical acclaim with the two records done like dinner since *Back in Black*. Angus and Malc knew it but would never concede it, doubling down on the wisdom of self-producing the last record and now the next one, promising that if the much-lauded Mutt Lange had got his way, *Back in Black* would have been even more polished than it was, the implication being that its stratospheric success isn't because of its big-shot outside producer.

Ergo, the band convened at Mountain Studios in Montreux, Switzerland, to a huge, round, freezing-cold room in a decommissioned casino to work on something that, as Malcolm struggled to articulate, was new and fresh and yet still stayed true to formula, one that was legendary for its compressed range and long rule book. Indeed, AC/DC were always part of the list of bands accused of doing the same thing over and over

Earthmovers in Hollywood, October 18, 1985, hours before their show at the L.A. Forum that evening.

Whole lotta Angus. Impersonators take the stage in Providence, Rhode Island, November 22, 1985.

again, along with Motörhead and the Ramones and to a lesser extent The Rolling Stones plus, for those who know the U.K. boogie legends, Status Quo. In fact, AC/DC and the Ramones are usually first and second examples of this uttered, then the debate begins after that. Then again, that was never a problem before, but it sure was now.

Indeed, there was nothing different about *Fly on the Wall*, other than the ushering in of a new drummer in Simon Wright (Phil Rudd had played on every AC/DC album thus far except for the debut). Writing took a long time, but the sessions went quickly, with Simon remarking that it felt like a band knocking off demos, casual, quick, easy, notwithstanding that the drummer in AC/DC has one of the easiest jobs in rock. The production credit would go to Angus and Malcolm this time, with Mark Dearnley—much less storied than Tony Platt—engineering.

If you thought *Flick of the Switch* was noisy, well, *Fly on the Wall*, issued June 28, 1985, was verging on a distorted mess, from the dry slap of the drums, through the buzz saw guitars, right up to Brian's throat-shredding, oxygen-challenged delivery of what is, on the main, a lunkheaded lump of lyrics. What stumbling drunk thought "Danger"

should be the album's first single is anybody's guess, although following up with "Sink the Pink" and "Shake Your Foundations" represented a two-pronged recovery of sorts, both of these capturing some of the hedonistic froth of the first wave hair metal music popular at the time.

In fact, more of a storyline than what singles were floated (then sunk) was the fact that the guys revisited the themed videos concept utilized across the *Flick of the Switch* clips. What they came up with was a twenty-seven-minute promotional video presenting six songs played in a cramped New York bar. Around the live performance buzzed the cartoon fly from the album cover plus the plotlines of a few characters, almost like a moving picture version of the six cover arts used for Led Zeppelin's *In Through the Out Door*. The mini-movie could be chopped up and played on MTV, all-powerful in 1985, though it was not like the unceremonious airings of these clips helped the record's anemic sales to any great effect.

Also, during the tour for the album, the band had to deal with the aforementioned "Night Prowler"/"Night Stalker" issue concerning serial killer Richard Ramirez, along with the attendant brouhaha over the "Satanic

A fan gets the point at the
Brendan Byrne Arena, East
Rutherford, New Jersey,
September 14, 1985.

panic" driving TV talk-show audiences insane at the time. In defense of his innocence, Angus had quipped, "I can't remember the last black mass I attended." Then there was Tipper Gore and the Parents Music Resource Center, who had a field day with "Sink the Pink" along with "Highway to Hell." On the road, AC/DC were followed by protesters from the religious right and had to fight meddling neighborhood groups and, in some cases, local governments just to put on their next show.

Despite the ill reception of a second—and arguably third—AC/DC album in a row, the band was still a major headline act, although ticket sales were light in some U.S. markets. Helping a bit was a secondary piece of product, the '74 Jailbreak EP, issued October 15, 1984. This consisted of four tracks from the band's Australian *High Voltage* debut recorded in 1974 but released in 1975, plus the flagship song "Jailbreak," which in fact was from 1976, albeit also, like the other songs, previously unreleased in the United States. As a single, the utilitarian, mid-level and old-school Bon Scott–era track made some noise, keeping the band in the news, not that finding the band's name in the mainstream press had been much of a problem ever since that cold night in London in February 1980.

Fly on the Wall managed a U.S. gold certification pretty much upon release but wouldn't see platinum until 2001. It stalled at #32 on Billboard, with none of the singles charting. Even if Malcolm, and to a lesser extent Angus, were always a pretty big part of the production process, they'd have to concede at this point that there is value in working with a professional producer, to dial in sounds, to be sure, but also to work the bullshit detector on the songs.

As much as Brian was inclined to dismiss the likes of Lange as "an expensive second set of ears," there was no denying the fact that the three records the band did with him sold more and were more seriously sold as completed albums than what they were now delivering muddy and rudderless. A rethink would be in order, with the band stumbling through one more record before recovering their sense of purpose and attendant sales domination in late 1990 and into 1991. Lo and behold, looking back and discovering that AC/DC had somewhat been relegated to the sidelines during what had essentially been a golden decade for the type of party-hardy hard rock they had originally made palatable to millions.

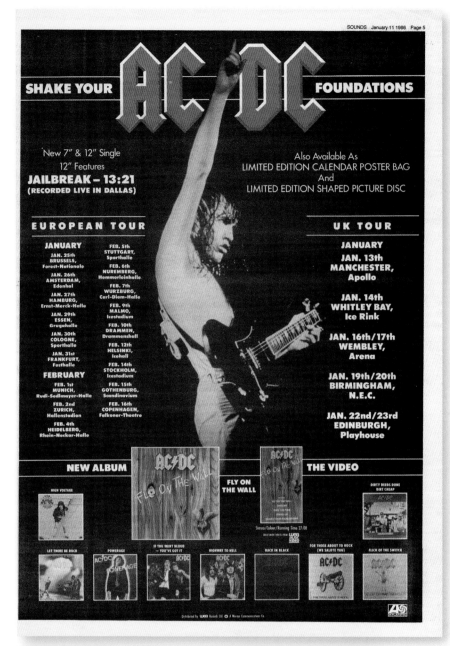

27
WAR MACHINE:
THE SOUNDTRACK/ HITS RELEASE, WHO MADE WHO

Proving the famed Woody Allen maxim, "Showing up is 80 percent of life," AC/DC found themselves doing soundtrack music for a box office bomb of a Stephen King movie and wound up with a five times platinum record in the process. Pertinently, to be sure, they showed up for that but also showed up with a few old songs. This is the band that famously vowed not to release a greatest hits record, but *Who Made Who* is sort of that and wouldn't be the last. They also showed up with a corker of a new track, around which is clumped these other songs. In other words, if you are the band behind *Back in Black*, stick around, do some stuff, and fortune may once again smile upon you, randomly.

Who Made Who, issued May 24, 1986, is, of course, called *Who Made Who* (and not *Greatest Hits*), and is fronted with an album cover that makes it look like a new studio album. It's got nine songs, so unlike *'74 Jailbreak* (which sold a million copies—another example of just showing up), it's a full-length album. "Sink the Pink" and "Shake Your Foundations" are there, boosting sales of *Fly on the Wall* or at least representing tacit support of the recent record, with their inclusions suggesting fans take a second look. The quiet and bluesy "Ride On," the only Bon Scott-era track on the album, loosely fits the *Maximum Overdrive* movie theme, so it's there but somewhat oddly.

Now, powering significantly the sales success of *Who Made Who* is the inclusion of "You Shook Me All Night Long," "Hells Bells," and "For Those About to Rock (We Salute You)." To be sure, that's only three smash hits, but the two *Fly on the Wall* tracks were also singles, so we're at least leaning into the idea of this being a hits package (and it's certainly a compilation).

This spread:
Wembley Arena,
London, January
16, 1986

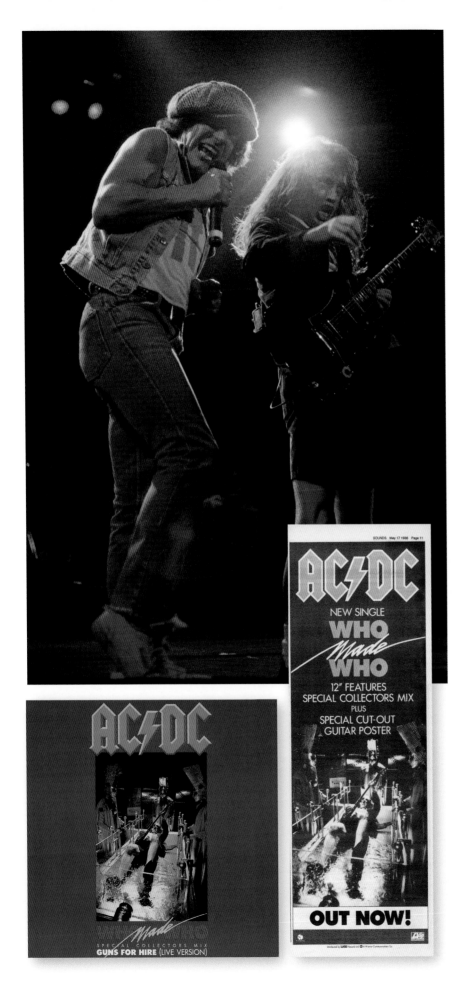

But wait, there's more . . . and by that I mean more hits. At the center of this record's success is its well-regarded title track. The band actually took it upon themselves to head back to Compass Point in Nassau to come up with the music for this project, working with Harry Vanda and George Young again—this is the first time Simon had met George—with Stephen King, a huge fan of the band, even coming down for a visit. Two of the new songs presented, "D.T." and "Chase the Ace," are instrumentals. They are barely acknowledged by the base, given that the last thing AC/DC can lay claim to being is a band that makes instrumentals, interesting or otherwise. These were written as the guys watched clips from the movie on TV screens and are thus the things on the record most faithful to the soundtrack album concept.

But "Who Made Who" is another story. Folks love this song, its signature widdly riff, its pounding modern rock beat, its melody, its chord changes, even its futuristic lyric, which had been sculpted directly for the movie, therefore adding to its sense of purpose and narrative. It's arguably the band's best song since take-your-pick from *Back in Black*, and it became a much-needed hit—aided and abetted by its strident clone concept video, directed by David Mallet—reaching #16 on the U.K. charts and #23 on the U.S. Mainstream Rock chart. What's more, it was an AC/DC set list staple across three ensuing tour cycles and remains highly regarded in the catalog to this day by ardent followers of the band.

Also fueling the success of *Who Made Who* was a commercial VHS video collection of the same name, offering, frankly, not that much more than the fleeting album—it sold over half a million copies, certifying gold in October 1986 in the video category. The results speak for themselves: The album would be certified platinum within a year, double in 1990, triple in 1993, and then five times platinum on the mass certification day done for AC/DC on January 22, 2001.

Unfortunately, "Who Made Who" would represent, arguably, the only true AC/DC classic constructed in the run of songs featuring Simon as the band's drummer. He'd be gone by the time the band thunk up "Thunderstruck," which represents the next time the guys would craft a classic, as well as the next time (depending on what you think of "This Means War") we'd get the widdly riff, on that occasion even more iconic and central to the song's premise than it is on "Who Made Who."

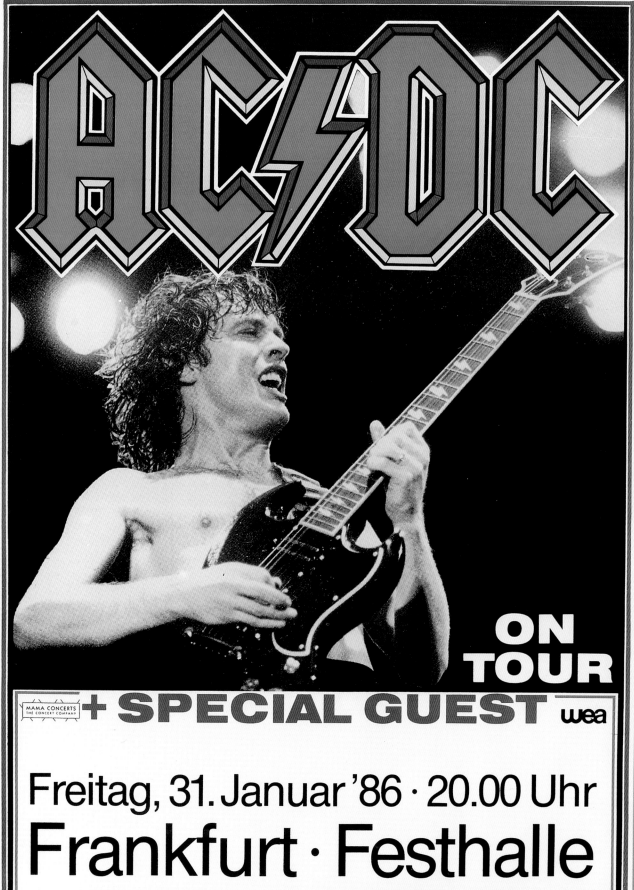

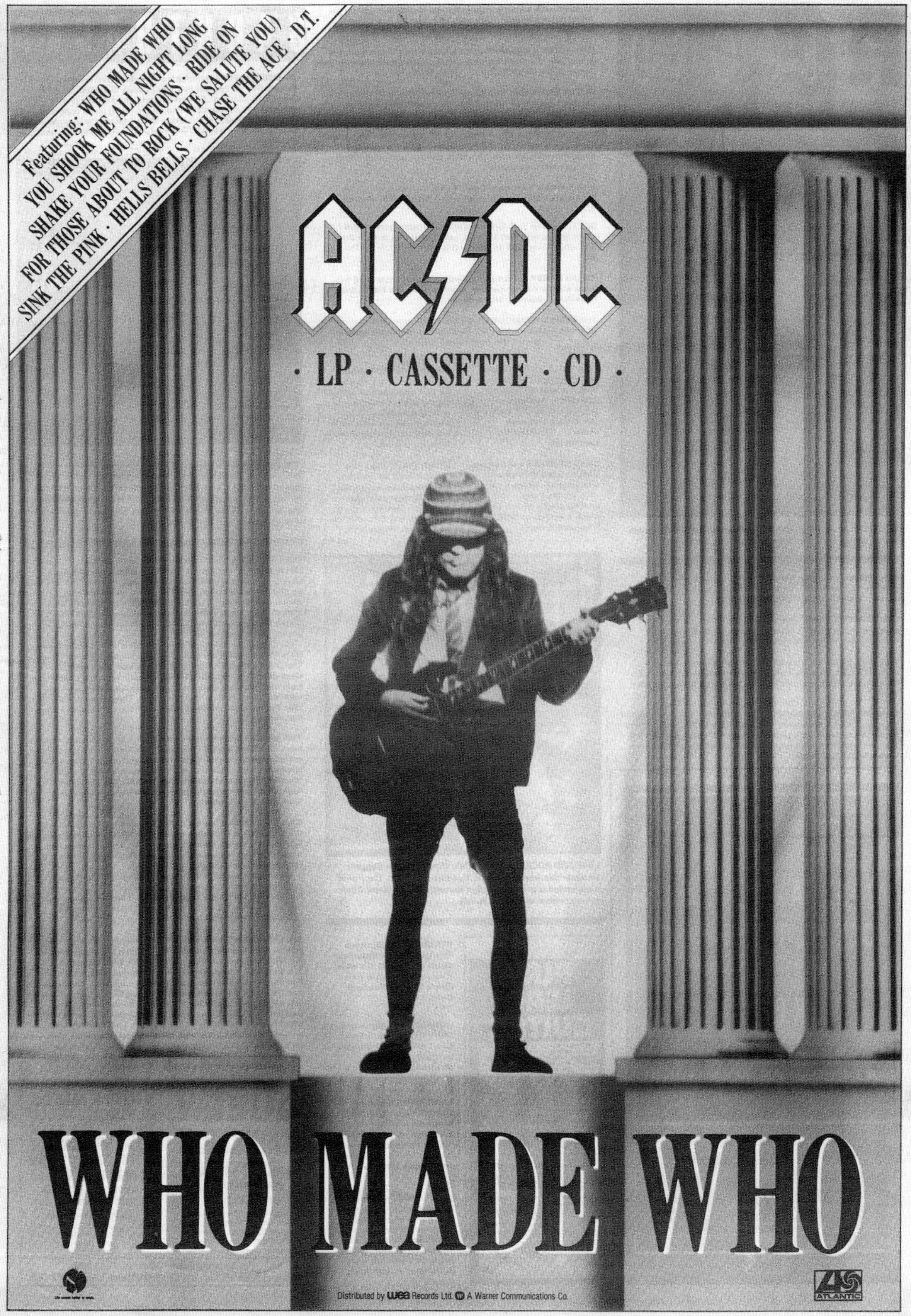

Featuring: WHO MADE WHO · YOU SHOOK ME ALL NIGHT LONG · SHAKE YOUR FOUNDATIONS · RIDE ON · FOR THOSE ABOUT TO ROCK (WE SALUTE YOU) · SINK THE PINK · HELLS BELLS · CHASE THE ACE · D.T.

AC/DC

· LP · CASSETTE · CD ·

WHO MADE WHO

Distributed by WEA Records Ltd. A Warner Communications Co.

28
SYSTEMS DOWN:
AC/DC ISSUE *BLOW UP YOUR VIDEO*

BLOW UP YOUR VIDEO

They'd been back to the Bahamas to try to recapture a bit of that *Back in Black* magic, and now it was time to go back to France, even if this time the guys would work far away from Paris, at Miraval in Correns in the south of France, where it may as well have been Nassau. The facilities were based in an old medieval complex, complete with tower and guest quarters. Opposite of Montreux, the sessions were scorching hot, with the place lacking air-conditioning (for relief, there was a golf course nearby).

Also in an attempt to get back on track, producing would be none other than Harry Vanda and George Young—again, they'd been there for the new *Who Made Who* material as well—ready to adjust the dials on a new batch of nineteen songs assembled from writing sessions at Nomis Studios in London, conducted in July 1987. But George was fed up with brother Malcolm's drinking by this point, even if the ol' Aussie team would manage to limp their way through the making of the next record, with Mal going into rehab partway through the subsequent touring cycle.

The resulting body of work, issued January 18, 1988, would go by the awkward title of *Blow Up Your Video*, which means what you think it would mean, AC/DC basically grumbling that videos are dumb and kids should be out seeing bands live, preferably AC/DC, who, one imagines by the sentiment, don't like making videos and therefore don't make good ones but do a good job on stage. The front cover of the record said as much as well, clumsily, with a blurry, bleached, badly lit Angus smashing his way out of a TV screen.

Once past the crap jacket, AC/DC do an adequate job of changing things up. There's bluesiness, novel song construction, arcane melodies, geometric riffs, and thoughtful lyrics with better vocals from Brian, but then again no standout hits and nothing exciting at the production end. To be sure, gone is the itchy surface grit of the last two records, sanded away by George and Vanda, but with it went dynamic range, most notably the top end. In essence, it was a case of guys from the 1970s navigating their way through late-1980s production tropes, resulting in the snapped-to-grid tightness we'd hear from Bruce Fairbairn and *The Razors Edge* but without that record's brightness and, more importantly, without the world-beating stadium rock ambition of its songs.

Despite the ardent search for something different, songs like "Meanstreak," "Ruff Stuff," and ill-advised second single "That's the Way I Wanna Rock N Roll" grasp at straws, telegraphing what would happen on *Stiff Upper Lip* and *Ballbreaker*, namely eccentric for eccentric's sake. Still, lead single "Heatseeker" satisfies, as does "Go Zone," ambled down a strident *For Those About to Rock* pathway, and "Kissin' Dynamite," with its angling toward *Flick of the Switch* cantankerousness. Then there's "Two's Up" and "Nick of Time," both set in a melodic space foreign

The band receives Australian platinum record awards for *Blow Up Your Video*, circa February 1988.

to AC/DC, and "This Means War," not the greatest song ever written but fast.

The public responded (perhaps still high on *Who Made Who* and more so "Who Made Who"), with the record reaching #2 on the U.K. charts and #12 on Billboard. *Blow Up Your Video* was also nominated for a Grammy in 1989, in a new category cooked up for hard rock. Famously, the award was won by Jethro Tull for *Crest of a Knave*, beating out favorite Metallica and their . . . *And Justice for All* album. But AC/DC were proposed as well, as was Jane's Addiction and Iggy Pop. Furthermore, *Blow Up Your Video* was simultaneously certified gold and platinum upon release, although it never got beyond that, underscoring the idea that any success the band was having was based on their live reputation (now we're back to the title) and the surprise breakout success of the band's oddball *Maximum Overdrive* soundtrack album.

George Young (left) and Harry Vanda (center) returned to the producers' chairs for *Blow Up Your Video*. They are seen here with the Easybeats in 1966.

29

TOUCH TOO MUCH:

MALCOLM ENTERS REHAB

The *Blow Up Your Video* tour began in Australia, with fourteen dates from February 1 through February 22, 1988, mostly multiple shows at the same venues and plagued by riots and arrests as AC/DC played to 130,000 fans rabid for their home-soil band who never seemed to be home. Next came an extensive European campaign in March and April. At this point, however, Malcolm had looked himself in the mirror and seen a full-blown alcoholic, one that, in his own words, was letting down the band as well as its fans.

For the ensuing U.S. campaign, running from May 3 through November 13, 1988, and supported by the likes of White Lion, Cinderella, and LA Guns, Malcolm would replace himself with his nephew, Stevie Young. The official reason given for the move was "exhaustion." Mal promptly returned to Sydney to begin recovery, attend AA meetings, reconnect with his two daughters and his wife Linda, dabble in horseracing, and of course do some writing for the next record.

As for his stand-in, Stevie is the son of Stephen Crawford Young Sr., who would sadly pass away the following year. Young Sr. was the eldest male among brothers Angus, Mal, George, and Alex. The family, unsurprisingly, was quite musical; and Stevie spent his life in various bands, most notable being Starfighters, who put out two well-regarded albums—*Starfighters* and *In-Flight Movie*—during the NWOBHM days, after Young had first emigrated to Australia like the rest, followed by a quick return to Scotland in 1970. Starfighters, who were based out of Birmingham, even opened for AC/DC on the *Back in Black* tour (as well as Ozzy Osbourne in 1982), with Stevie known to travel with AC/DC in the late 1970s.

The brothers Young, Australia 1987

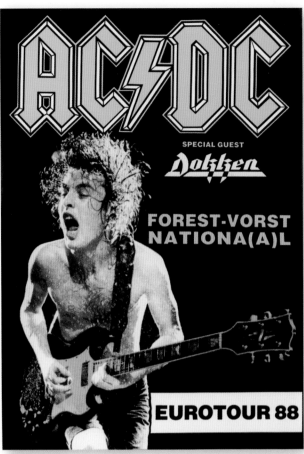

He was the perfect choice for another reason as well—AC/DC prided themselves on a sense of family, valuing the shared blood and shared experiences that are the legacy of the Young clan's colorful past. Additionally, Angus is on record articulating how special Stevie always was as a Malcolm-type rhythm guitarist, underscoring how rare it is to find someone who takes to rhythm so deftly, even though Angus was aware that, like Malcolm, Stevie could do so much more. Dependable as a worker, as part of the family and rock-solid as a rhythm section collaborator with Simon and Cliff, Stevie was a choice almost of destiny.

Given that there was no internet, coupled with the insular and secretive nature of AC/DC when it came to communication with the outside world, many fans witnessing the band on the U.S. tour likely had no clue that Mal had been deputized by a relative. After all, the focus was on Angus, who began the show leaping out of a missile that rose from the middle of the stage as the band collapsed into "Heatseeker." And if you weren't watching a very long-haired Angus crisscross the stage, hoping and praying that his very white and knobby knees would last the two hours, you were watching Brian, shimmying at the lip, mic clenched in one hand and fist clenched in the other, folding himself into what were widely considered superlative vocal performances from this legend who, frankly, never made it easy on himself.

Concerning Stevie, he bore a resemblance to Malcolm (despite being taller), kept his hair hanging over his face like the boss, and even played the same distinctive Gretsch Jet Firebirds—and by choice. Stevie also played the role well, mostly headbanging away close to the right of Simon and his kit, albeit stepping up for backing vocals, which merely added to his worth.

It would be two years before AC/DC played live again, by which time Malcolm would have kicked the booze and rejoined the fold. However, as fate would have it, this wouldn't be the last time Stevie would be called upon to replace the beloved patriarch of the band.

30

THUNDERSTRUCK:

THE COMEBACK ALBUM, THE RAZORS EDGE

Come time for the next record, Malcolm would return but AC/DC would lose Simon. It was a confluence of events, really. AC/DC were no longer the tight unit they had been. Brian for years had been living in Fort Myers, Florida; and now he was joined by Cliff, who was going there from Hawaii. Angus was in the Netherlands, and Malcolm was back and forth between Australia and London.

Simon, notably, had moved to Fresno, California, from Manchester. At this point, with AC/DC not touring in 1989, Simon took up the offer to play with Ronnie James Dio, whom he had long admired, ending up playing on the Dio record *Lock Up the Wolves*, issued in May 1990. At first the idea was that he'd feature as a guest, but it would solidify into much more from there. For their part, Mal and Angus felt slighted, remarking that Simon never warmed to the guys anyway, keeping to himself his whole time in the band, never saying much more than hello or goodbye. As for Simon, he had said that he just wanted to work, while also expressing that he wanted to spread his wings as a drummer and play some more elaborate material.

A few demos were banged together, but soon Simon was out, replaced by Chris Slade of Manfred Mann fame but also The Firm, Gary Moore, and, in the mid-1960s, Tom Jones! Malcolm had spotted Slade playing with Moore (the two bands shared management), and it was a quick grab, really, with Slade first called in to accompany the band in Brighton as they wrote songs but not asked to join officially at this point.

Things got more serious at Windmill Studios in Ireland, the band working with engineer Ian Taylor while awaiting Vanda and Young to join them as the project's production team, which didn't pan out due to personal issues the elder Young had to take care of. And so what was to become *The Razors Edge* (sic—no apostrophe!) would get constructed during a six-week set of sessions at Little Mountain Studios in Vancouver, after a quick trip by Mal to check out the situation. Producing would be Bruce Fairbairn, who had been generating smash-hit records as of late with Bon Jovi and Aerosmith, having first hit the big time with his slick productions for local act Loverboy.

The resulting body of work, twelve songs long, reflecting a nudging of the band into the CD age, would represent the tightest, brightest sound—in fact, shockingly sharp at the drum position—applied to the band since *Highway to Hell*, with all of the hallmarks of a Mutt Lange whip-snapping at the arrangement end attendant as well, unsurprising given Fairbairn's notoriously strong opinions and refusal to be pushed around by rock stars.

Additional drama came with the fact that Brian, preoccupied by divorce proceedings with his wife, Carol, bowed out of writing lyrics for the new record, with the credits for every song going to Angus and Mal. In a sort of one-and-done mirroring of what just happened to Simon, Brian would never write lyrics for the band again, every record moving forward being packed with songs credited to the Young brothers and no one else. Brian was known to express relief at having the pressure off his back, but one wonders what he would have done had he'd known it would be forever.

NOW THERE ARE TWO THINGS TO BE AFRAID OF ON APRIL 15TH.

1040 Department of the Treasury—Internal Revenue Service
For the year January 1–December 31, 1990, or other tax year beginning
U.S. Individual Income Tax Return **1990**
383 20824 - 2675

"Are You Ready"

If you're not too busy hiding your assets this April, look for the latest super single
multiplatinum album
THE RAZORS EDGE (91413).
It's a blast.

AC/DC

Produced by Bruce Fairbairn.
Management: Stewart Young/Steve Barnett for Part Rock Management, Ltd.

The flagship track on *The Razors Edge* would forever be opening salvo "Thunderstruck," with its circular and hypnotic note-dense guitar lick and its slow-build arrangement. But the hits kept coming, with the melodic and Stones-y "Moneytalks" becoming the band's highest-charting hit ever in the United States, at #23, and serving as the platform for the main piece of imagery associated with the album and tour, Angus on various currencies. The AC/DC guys weren't exactly broke, but they've always remembered where they came from and were all too happy to play the underdog, which meant, as they did in this hummable track, complaining about rich people. Also a flagship song was "Are You Ready," a menacing rocker that brightens at the pre-chorus and brightens further at the chorus, with its title sentiment found to work well at sporting events, and so there it can be heard regularly to this day (along with "Thunderstruck").

Speaking of dark, the album's title track is one of the band's most malevolent-sounding songs in years, with Angus intimating that the lyric refers to dark storm clouds, war, and maybe even, at a stretch, Armageddon. Lightening things up is the notorious "Mistress for Christmas," written about Donald Trump and which opened with sleigh bells, AC/DC being Johnny-on-the-spot with a new carol, given the record's September 21, 1990, release date. The balance of the songs are frankly sent over the top by the energy and economy of their performances, coupled with the hard sheen of the production palette utilized, especially at the bass drum but also the snare.

The Razors Edge would vault to #2 and represent a true renaissance for the band, extending the magic touch Bruce Fairbairn was having on bands' fortunes at the time. It was easy to celebrate AC/DC again, without reserve, without having to argue the case too hard. Viewed another way, each of the last four albums have sizeable contingents of superfans, but with The Razors Edge, AC/DC were cool again for everyone. Within eighteen months, the album would be certified triple platinum, en route to its current status at an impressive five times platinum, notably certifying higher than For Those About to Rock, the record floated upon the tsunami of success that was Back in Black. This also represented a fivefold jump from the band's last album of the 1980s, a decade that began meteoric but then had our heroes grinding through the ensuing years as something approximating the status of mere mortals.

PART 3
LEGACY

Mal and Angus,
becoming elder
statesmen of rock

31

MONEY MADE:

BACK IN BLACK CERTIFIED 10X PLATINUM

It's reassuring on some level that when Bon Scott went to his grave on February 19, 1980, he died with the knowledge that his lovable band of rogues, AC/DC, was on its way to some level of notoriety, given that *Highway to Hell* had been certified by the RIAA as gold for U.S. sales of over 500,000 copies on December 6 of the previous year.

Bon's death in a cold car was a shocking news story to be sure, but again, this was a band already on its way, and before the issue of *Back in Black* in July 1980, *Highway to Hell* had already gone platinum a month after Bon's demise. So to recap, by the summer of 1980, the legend of Bon Scott had already become firmly established, AC/DC already had a platinum album, and now there was a further couple of new cycles with respect to the band having a new singer as well as a new album.

Fortunate to the trending career trajectory, *Back in Black* delivered the goods, generating instant appeal fueled by a trio of big anthemic hits in the stomping title track, the brooding "Hells Bells," and the crossover pop seduction of "You Shook Me All Night Long." On the strength of all of the above, the album coasted to a simultaneous gold and platinum RIAA certification on October 13, 1980.

Requests for further certification would be delayed as the band toured hard, worked quite soon on a follow-up, and at the same time, as discussed, experienced issues with management, declining to re-sign with Steve Leber

and David Krebs, who had worked with the band during the *Highway to Hell* album and tour cycle through to the summer of 1982.

Back in Black would be certified five times platinum on October 30, 1984, after the issue of two more studio albums, *For Those About to Rock* in 1981 and *Flick of the Switch* in 1983. And then the record just kept selling and selling. I've often argued that the tours for these couple of records and perhaps the next two as well were essentially extensions of the *Back in Black* tour, given that after the initial flurry of sales for *For Those About to Rock* in late 1981 and early 1982, *Back in Black* was essentially regularly outselling the band's 1981, 1983, 1985, and 1988 records throughout the rest of the decade.

The album would next be certified at nine times platinum on October 4, 1990, and then ten times platinum three weeks later. However, this technically did not represent diamond status for *Back in Black*, given that the diamond designation did not come into being until 1999—the gold award had been invented in 1958, modified in 1975, with platinum declared in 1976 and multiplatinum in 1984. The next call for certification wasn't until 1996, when the album was certified twelve times platinum, with the album achieving nineteen times platinum on January 22, 2001, which, one supposes, technically represents the record certifying as diamond.

Interestingly, however, outside of Canada and the band's home base of Australia, the album performed like a regular ol' successful album, notching gold through low multiplatinum numbers all over Europe, including the United Kingdom. Additionally, *Back in Black* only got to #4 on the Billboard charts, albeit ending the year at a strong #7, perhaps telegraphing its staying power.

On December 6, 2019, the album was certified twenty-five times platinum, which is essentially multi-diamond, putting the record in a rarefied space, in fact situating it as the fourth-biggest-selling album of all time in the United States, after, in order, The Eagles' *Their Greatest Hits (1971–1975)*, Michael Jackson's *Thriller*, and The Eagles' *Hotel California*. While the Michael Jackson record has proven to be roughly equal to *Back in Black* with respect to song streams, a quick calculation using Spotify numbers would suggest that the AC/DC album continues to fire the imagination of future generations at a far greater pace and intensity than does the peaceful, easy yacht-rock sounds of The Eagles.

Enjoying a bite — and multiplatinum success—1990

32

GO ZONE:

HEADLINING RUSSIA'S FIRST-EVER OPEN-AIR ROCK FESTIVAL

Long story, but the lesson learned is that when the going gets tough, metal takes over. Monsters of Rock took place at the Tushino Airfield on September 28, 1991, after a previously planned show featuring Peter Gabriel, U2, the Eurythmics, Bob Dylan, and The Rolling Stones had wilted due to headliners dropping out one by one. Mind you, this was all taking place as the Soviet Union was going through its death throes, in transition from Gorbachev to Yeltsin and the empire's ultimate dissolution on December 26, 1991.

So it's a miracle that any concert by westerners could have taken place at all, much less a massive heavy metal onslaught in front of 500,000 to 700,000 rampaging youth (entry was free and counting heads was hard), there to witness, first, Pantera (with only *Cowboys from Hell* under their belts as a major label release at that point) and The Black Crowes followed by local rockers Electro Shock Therapy. Next came Metallica, playing what is considered the greatest show of their storied career, fired up by the release of their self-titled "black album" a month previous; and then, as night enshrouded the teeming mass of bodies, our headlining heroes of wild and free music, AC/DC.

An edict was put in place to make disappear the paperwork and layers of bureaucracy previously thought insurmountable for such an event to take place in the Soviet Union. In fact, the extravaganza had been the brainchild of Time Warner, who, in the end, had wound up making $80 million on the distribution rights associated with the

resulting *For Those About to Rock* documentary generated by the event. The lofty aim beyond the business venture side of it was to celebrate the Soviet people becoming free, embracing democracy, and, frankly, defeating Communism, a decades-long goal of the West and especially America.

U.S. marines were employed to commandeer twenty-four truckloads of sound and lighting and get the nine-story stage built. Usually a concert of this magnitude took months of planning and preparation, but Monsters of Rock Moscow was pulled together in three weeks. Come the day of the event, a consortium of private and government security 11,000 strong took over, keeping control over a crowd that wasn't allowed to buy alcohol on-site but was allowed to bring it in, with thousands well liquored up and ready to fight before they arrived—and fight they did, unsurprisingly, at the outset, spurred on by the extreme aggression of Pantera firing on all cylinders.

AC/DC opened their momentous two-hour set with their world-beating new hit "Thunderstruck," following up with "Shoot to Thrill" and "Back in Black." Next was the semi-obscure *Let There Be Rock* track "Hell Ain't a Bad Place to Be," followed by the brand-new and very fast "Fire Your Guns" and then the truly archival "Jailbreak" and "The Jack." "Moneytalks" would be the third and last of the new songs before a cavalcade of expected hits filled the back half of the set, culminating in "For Those About to Rock (We Salute You)," a fitting message for the night and maybe even more so given its artillery subplot. Two

performances from the occasion would be added to the 1992 *Live* album, with three more being tossed onto the *Backtracks* box set compilation.

The miracle of Monsters of Rock Moscow is that there were no reported fatalities. In fact, despite reports of police bashing heads and perhaps going overboard on arrests (Moscow City police recorded fifty-one people requiring hospitalization, and the local drunk tanks filled up fast), it was the security detail that was instrumental in preventing what could have been a wide-scale disaster of people being crushed given the multitude of fans constantly surging to the front of the stage. Amazingly, it had taken a flurry of batons to quell the crushing waves of humanity, but as the day wore on, it was as if a mass collective consciousness had taken over, with the crowd correcting and essentially learning on the spot how to get to the end of a night of "festival seating" without death. AC/DC had, in fact, just dealt with such a situation when, earlier in the year, three fans were killed at a show in Salt Lake City, crushed as Angus launched into the opening riff of "Thunderstruck." No doubt, this was on the minds of the festival headliners as the opening strains of that same anthem for the ages echoed across the airfield, lighting fire to a show that would be the biggest concert in AC/DC history.

This spread: Monsters of Rock, Moscow, September 28, 1991. Half a million people jammed an airfield to see AC/DC, the Black Crowes, and Metallica play at the Soviet Union's biggest western rock concert, touted as a gift to Russian youth for their resistance to the previous month's coup.

BACK IN BRONZE:

MIKE MILSOM AND THE HELL'S BELL

AC/DC is famed for many things, but one of those is a wrecking ball. Another one is cannons. But the mother of all "heavy metal" props is the band's doomful tolling bell, heard before it was seen, on *Back in Black*'s first song "Hells Bells." The bell tolls for Bon Scott, respectfully, but it also tolls more literally in support of this sullen and slouching heavy rock anthem. As the song and album (and in concert) would grow to near mythical iconic proportions, well, Hell's Bell now tolls for the opposition sports team in your arena, as the home side hears confirmation over the PA of a favorable shift in momentum, the local heroes now drawing strength from AC/DC to finish off the enemy.

But they're really drawing strength from a chap named Mike Milsom. "I was bellmaster at John Taylor & Co, Bellfounders, at Loughborough in the UK," explained Milsom, in an introductory 2020 email to the author, after he had purchased my 2017 book *AC/DC: Album by Album*. "I cast and tuned the Hell's Bell and tolled it for the recording that went onto the album. Initially the request was for a large bell note 'C' but the six weeks we were given to produce the bell ruled this out. Also, this bell would have weighed two U.K. tons, which was considered to be too heavy to use on stage at live concerts. Consequently, we cast the bell that is note 'E,' 48 inches or 121 centimetres in diameter and weighing 1.03 U.K. tons or 2,318 pounds or 1,051 kilograms. They also didn't want the bell to be grey, so it was painted gold. Plus we had to include a large, polished-up AC/DC logo that would nicely reflect the lights."

Engineer Tony Platt
at the foundry

"A recording was needed forthwith," continues Milsom, "as the album was being mixed in New York. As soon as it was tuned, Tony Platt came to the bellfoundry with an Airstream caravan that was a mobile recording studio from Manor Recording Studios that belonged to Richard Branson and Virgin Records. Tony used 16 microphones recording onto 24 channels and the tape was immediately flown to New York for Mutt Lange.

"My tolling of the bell was dropped down in pitch to 'A' to make it sound more majestic for the album and live concerts."

"There is a longstanding myth regarding an attempt to record the four-ton 'Denison' bass bell at the Loughborough WWI Memorial Carillon, which has 47 bells cast by Taylor's in 1923. This was discussed with Tony Platt as the recording was so urgently needed, but I advised against it, and it was discounted. Vehicle access to the carillon tower was difficult and the bell chamber is 140 feet off the ground. They actually tried it, as I was off on holiday, but the constant cooing from pigeons and then their flying off when the bell was struck, along with the traffic noise, was impossible to overcome. In the end we recorded it at the foundry, which I opened up late at night so it would be quiet. The bell had to be struck precisely in four places, with the effect complicated by the AC/DC logo putting the bell out of balance, causing a slow, pulsing sound, which in the bell business is called wobble. In retrospect I should have asked for a performance fee! I hope you may find this information interesting. Regards, Mike Milsom."

Indeed, I had, thanking Milsom, who followed up with this: "A quick correction. I have backtracked to find where I got the info about the mobile recording studio that Tony Platt brought to the bellfoundry. It actually came from Ronnie Lane who acquired the airstream caravan in 1972, and it is often referred to as LMS, or Lane Mobile Studio. It was fitted out by audio engineer Ron Nevison and used by a large number of people until it was sold in 1982. There is a photograph of it on the album cover of Ronnie's 1976 *One for the Road* album. Regards, Mike."

For those who want more of the tale, Milson has written a memoir called *Bells & Bellfounding: A History, Church Bells, Carillons, John Taylor & Co., Bellfounders, Loughborough, England*, from which he then sent to the author an excerpt. In it (after a cheery "I am delighted that you like my story, so here is the next bit!"), we learn that AC/DC kept breaking or misplacing the six hammers supplied and used to ring the bell, so John Taylor & Co. had to keep making new ones for them. Then Angus had requested that the bell swing above the band whilst they are on stage, so Taylor had to design a special fastening system with a motor and chain drive. Milson then had to solve the problem of the sound matching the swing, which is quite ingenious and takes up a long paragraph in the book—bottom line, a button could be pushed manually by a roadie at the opportune moment. In the end it turned out that the swinging motion put too much force on the supporting gantries and the idea would have to be quashed. Taylor & Co. continued to receive work from AC/DC over the years repainting the bell, with the company even receiving a commission from Malcolm Young to make him a scaled-down replica, reportedly used to replace a candelabra in his dining room.

33

KICKED IN THE TEETH:

A SECOND LIVE ALBUM, SIMPLY CALLED *LIVE*

Riding high off the success of *The Razors Edge*, AC/DC surely picked the right time to issue their first live album since way back before they ever had a single hit album, squeezing in *If You Want Blood* after *Powerage* and before *Highway to Hell*. What's amusing is that there'd be little excitement on the streets for the album, not because it wasn't appreciated but because everybody and their devil dog had seen AC/DC do what they do here at some point across the Brian Johnson era, now a decade on. What's more, it's not like we'd be getting obscure covers or vastly different interpretations of the band's own songs, nor even that imaginative of a set list. There were just too many hits to get through, especially given how long it had been since a live album.

So the unimaginatively named *Live* arrived October 27, 1992, in two versions separated by a few weeks, a fourteen-track single-disc package and a twenty-three-track double package with the added designation, "Special Collector's Edition" (also included with the latter was an "Angus buck," basically a small U.S. dollar bill featuring Angus and a big AC/DC logo, badly cropped with full-color printing on only one side).

Typical of the AC/DC cone of silence, there weren't many details about the performances on the album concerning where they were recorded (using either the Manor mobile or the Plant mobile) or the fact that the production credit to Bruce Fairbairn and the mix credits to Ken Lomas and his assistant Mike Plotnikoff (a British Columbia Doukhobor of lineage, just like me!) included guitar overdubs and fixed vocals. Dispensing with the negatives, it was unfortunate that the crowds were allowed to fade out at the end of each track and back in for the next one, a jarring distraction that killed any illusion that we were hearing an unmolested AC/DC concert.

But yes, past these points, *Live* is a corker of a live album, recorded with edge and aggression, avoiding the mistakes of bloated hockey barn sound made across most 1980s live albums from 1970s bands shoved out the door by the likes of Rush, Blue Öyster Cult, Thin Lizzy, Judas Priest, and Scorpions, to name but a few. Some of the credit should go to the fact that overseeing things was Bruce Fairbairn, who brought

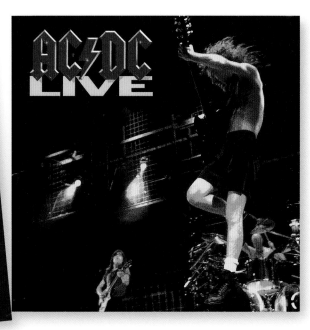

these visceral characteristics to the last studio album, along with Chris Slade, who somehow drums more angular than does Phil Rudd, which changes ever so slightly the complexion of some of these songs.

The single-CD edition of the album is all business, offering hit after hit, with two of them ("Moneytalks" and opener "Thunderstruck") from the most recent album, three of them very early days ("The Jack," "T.N.T.," and "Dirty Deeds Done Dirt Cheap"), and only one song ("Heatseeker") from any of the three 1980s albums that didn't sell so hot.

The two-CD edition (originally issued in the ridiculed CD longbox format) adds "Sin City," "That's the Way I Wanna Rock N Roll," a one-minute traditional "Bonny" sing-along, "Fire Your Guns," "The Razors Edge," and "Are You Ready" from the recent spread, resulting in a total of five *The Razors Edge* songs on the live album. Most pertinently, however, is the huge pile of Angus Young guitar soloing on offer, heard most profusely across "Jailbreak," "Let There Be Rock," and "High Voltage," which together add up to an unexpected thirty-seven minutes of stretching out, with, granted, "High Voltage" also burning time with a crowd participation piece marbled into the blues jam and actually quite amusing vocal vamping from Brian, who doesn't fail to entertain with his asides throughout the record.

As for shows of origin, aside from celebrations of Monsters of Rock UK and Monsters of Rock Moscow, the dates were typical AC/DC gigs, captured with the mobiles at the NEC in Birmingham, the Scottish Event Campus Centre in Glasgow, and the Northlands Coliseum in Edmonton, Alberta, Canada. Amusingly, Brian's "We've got a song for you, Dublin" preceding "Sin City" is a triple mistake of sorts. First off, he said that to a crowd in Belfast. Second, what he actually said in Dublin was "Okay, Dublin, we've got a song especially for you." Third, this performance of "Sin City" is from Birmingham.

Live did good business out in the marketplace, reaching double platinum on September 14, 1993, and triple platinum January 30, 2001. Certifications for the Collector's Edition all took place in 2001, at that point the album designated gold, platinum, and double platinum simultaneously, although double CDs get counted twice. Like I say, there really wasn't a great deal of excitement for the album at the time, and again, I figure that's because there was really no mystery to AC/DC live for a wide swath of the hard rock populace. Plus the studio versions were just fine, and there was no shortage of those on classic rock radio. In any event, *Live* would have to last us. Not only was the album not supported by a tour; there would, in fact, be no AC/DC concert appearances for another four years and no new studio album for three.

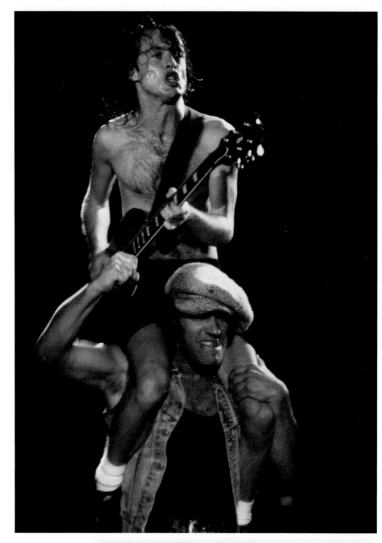

AC/DC stacking the deck in Sacramento, June 15, 1991

34
RUFF STUFF:
AC/DC ISSUE
BALLBREAKER

Before the unplanned semi-retirement of AC/DC through 1993 and 1994, a bug had been put in Malcolm's ear at a 1991 show in New Zealand by a former compatriot named Phil Rudd. It seems that a rehabilitation of sorts had happened, and Phil figured he might be of use to the lads again if the opportunity ever become available. Soon Chris Slade was out, fired for not much reason, and Phil hired, also for not much more reason other than Mal's opinion that Phil had created the signature AC/DC drum sound and that it was hard to get out of anybody but Phil. Slade was so incensed by being ousted that he quit the drum trade for three years—amusingly, the tables would be turned when Slade replaced Phil twenty years later, albeit only for the tour dates in support of *Rock or Bust*, with Phil back yet again in time for the *Power Up* album.

In 1993, famed Los Angeles producer Rick Rubin had taken the production credit on a surprise one-off minor hit for AC/DC, a trundling tank of a track called "Big Gun," which was the first of twelve tracks on the soundtrack album for the Arnold Schwarzenegger movie *Last Action Hero*. The movie was a blockbuster, the album went platinum, and "Big Gun" got to #65 on the main Billboard chart but #1 on the Mainstream Rock chart and #5 in Canada. Rubin was, in fact, an AC/DC nut, proving as much when he essentially converted The Cult into an AC/DC clone band, producing the hit *Electric* album for Ian Astbury and Billy Duffy back in 1987.

So it seemed sensible that AC/DC might try constructing a whole record with Rubin, with the team assembling at Power Station in New York to try to make it happen. Unfortunately, the band couldn't get an adequate drum sound there, with Rubin putting Phil and his kit in a tent and then trying all manner of absorbers and deadeners on the walls. With fifty hours of tape filled, the guys gave up, jetting across the country and back to Rick's home base of Los Angeles (bad idea), setting up at Ocean Way Studios where five tense months were spent assembling the new album.

As engineer Mike Fraser explained to me, "He was never there. Never in the studio. So that was interesting. We started off . . . Rick had picked out a studio in New York to work at and after six weeks we ended up with nothing. Not one thing on tape that we could use. Just a nightmare. So we went to LA and did the whole thing there. I remember once in New York, I think just because tension was running high, Malcolm and Angus had a go at it, and I guess it was just a big screaming match, maybe almost came to blows. We all just left the studio and they were there for three hours, yelling and screaming, throwing chairs or I don't know what [laughs]. But you know, once that's said, then everything's cool. Some of the crew said that happens once in a while with those two, just because they're so passionate."

As Fraser indicates, Rubin (as Rubin does) was often absent from the sessions, stealing away to work on the Red Hot Chili Peppers' *One Hot Minute* album. When he was around, he'd put the band through upwards of fifty takes, reminding Mal and Angus of the hell they'd gone through with Mutt Lange at the start of his descent into mental production madness. Speaking volumes is the fact that in the end, the co-production credit on the new record went to Fraser (Bruce Fairbairn's more-than-skilled right-hand man), letting us all know who really got this project to the finish line at the technical end.

To be sure, an album got done; but *Ballbreaker*, issued September 26, 1995, lacks any of the giddy electric excitement Rubin generated for the likes of Slayer, Wolfsbane, The Cult, The Four Horsemen, Trouble, Masters of Reality, or Danzig. A mere mean/medium/average of the sound pictures blessing the Rubin records for those bands might have turned *Ballbreaker*, with this precise deck of eleven songs, into the most ass-kicking AC/DC album since *Flick of the Switch*. But it isn't that, because this supercharged sound characteristic of Rubin's hard rock productions inside of this magical window never gets applied to AC/DC.

And yet, despite possessing the sonics of *For Those About to Rock* crossed with *Blow Up Your Video*, *Ballbreaker* is considerably entertaining, daring in its simplicity, its pregnant pauses, and in no mood to come off as heavy metal, with the guitars oddly clean and restrained, allowing the songs to breathe. Best of the bunch are flagship boogie rocker and album opener "Hard as a Rock" (which dates back to the *Who Made Who* sessions), bookended by the menacing title track closing the album. In between there's "The Furor" and "Burnin' Alive," both dark of lyric and chord progression, with the latter being about the 1993 siege in Waco, Texas, in which seventy-six followers of religious fanatic David Koresh were killed. "Boogie Man" is a rare rote blues for the band, while "Caught with Your Pants Down," late in the sequence, is both up-tempo and traditionally lascivious, rivaling "Cover You in Oil" and the title track for incendiary wordage.

The new prop for the tour (and for the "Hard as a Rock" video) was a swinging wrecking ball, and with that, the band appointed itself well on the ensuing near year of dates, driven through each song by a rejuvenated and bespectacled Phil and Brian singing great, confounding science year after year.

Ballbreaker pretty quickly found its platinum certification, with the record being designated double platinum in 2001. Lacking in hits (despite being promoted heavily), the record's success in the stores could be chalked up to pent-up demand, with fans parched for AC/DC product. In retrospect, little did we know at the time that the "For Those About to Rock" explosions marking the end of AC/DC's show in Auckland, New Zealand, on November 16, 1991, would be the last time the guys would treat the band like a full-time job. It's a harsh assessment to be sure, but maybe the passive, relaxed nature of *Ballbreaker* betrays this fact, that AC/DC were about to become hobbyists.

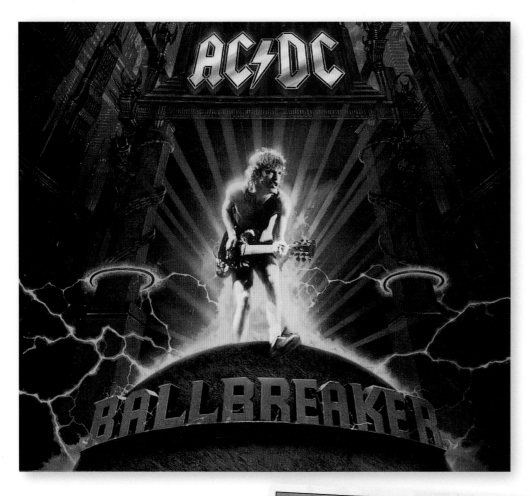

The new album featuring

"HARD AS A ROCK"

Produced by Rick Rubin
Co-produced by Mike Fraser

On EastWest Records America compact discs, sesec cassettes and records
World Wide Web: http://www.elektra.com

Plaza De Toros De Las Ventas, MADRID | FILMED LIVE ON SUPER 16mm FILM
LOS DIAS 10 DE JULIO DE 1996   EastWest Records America #40192-3

35

UP TO MY NECK IN YOU:

THE *BONFIRE* BOX SET

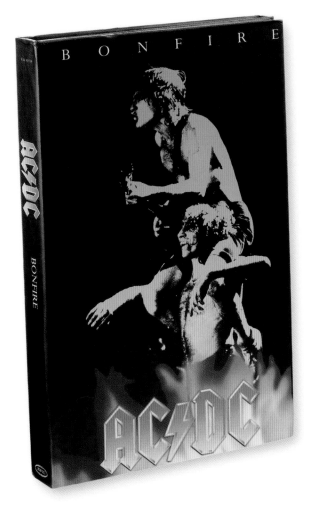

The *Bonfire* box, approximately timed through its release date of November 18, 1997, to celebrate what would have been Bon Scott's birthday, finally finds AC/DC's consortium of business interests opening the vault doors, revealing—or allowing—not a lot, not a little, but landing somewhere in the middle.

The five-CD package kicks off with the *Live from the Atlantic Studios* set from December 7, 1977. Sound quality is middling and the performances somewhat modest, as the band takes their dead-simple brand of old-timey music to a small audience forced to re-examine how many action points they needed out of a live performance. Fortunately this was post *Let There Be Rock*, so there are some meaner, less lean numbers included, such as "Hell Ain't a Bad Place to Be," "Dog Eat Dog," and "Whole Lotta Rosie."

Creating quite the contrast is the next set, two discs of the band recorded live at the Pavillon de Paris, in Paris, France, on December 9, 1979, two months before Bon's death across the channel. At this point *Highway to Hell* was four months runnin' hot, so we got to hear "Shot Down in Flames," "Girls Got Rhythm," the title track to the record, and most delectably, "Walk All Over You," which arrives with a bit of a limp, due to Phil drumming it closer to a halting four-on-the-floor compared to the monstrous groove we hear on the studio album. "Girls Got Rhythm" and "Shot Down in Flames," on the other hand, get the true-to-original four-on-the-floor beats we hear on the record; and they both pound proudly, made all the more impressive by the huge, distorted guitars captured in this set. In fact, when we get to "Hell Ain't a Bad Place to Be" and "Sin City," the distortion dominates to the point of technical malfunction, although this is fixed for the rest of the set. Topping things off is a thespian performance out of Bon that demonstrates why folks call him one of the best front men of all time. To be sure, we can't see him, but we actually can, because this is, in effect, the soundtrack album to *Let There Be Rock: The Movie, Live in Paris*, the concert movie released back in 1980 to little fanfare.

Disc four is the jewel in the jewel cases. "Dirty Eyes" is a proper, finished recording of an alternate version of "Whole Lotta Rosie," complete with different lyrics and noticeable divergences in the musical arrangement. "Touch Too Much" is, in fact, a whole new unissued song, sharing only the title with the *Highway to Hell* classic. Then there's a well-recorded (and slower) demo version of "If You Want Blood" with different lyrics, followed by the delightful "Back Seat Confidential," an early playful version of "Beatin' Around the Bush," and yet another all-new song, "Get It Hot," which has nothing to do with the *Highway to Hell* song, again, other than the title.

Next are a couple sort of orphaned live tracks plus the quaint "School Days" from the Australian *High Voltage* debut. Disc four closes on a downer, offering "It's a Long Way to the Top" (Australian version, i.e., ten seconds longer) and the regular version of "Ride On," reminding us that these compilations are compiled by people that don't put much thought into things. Amplifying that sentiment, there are a few undocumented interview snippets tucked onto the end of "Ride On."

But disc five is the one that really confused and ticked off fans: It's the *Back in Black* album start to finish, which was undoubtedly in the collections of every last punter who ponied up to the counter in 1997 to purchase *Bonfire*. Granted, it was presented remastered, but still, this is a detail that impressed few but the hardcore.

Besides the music, the package offered a forty-eight-page booklet stuffed with Bon Scott-era pictures, a perfunctory essay, a pile of stand-alone band quotes, and adequately explanatory track notes. Included also was a large sticker, a tiny AC/DC logo decal, a keychain, and a

Bon Scott, elegantly repackaged

two-sided poster featuring a repeat of the cover of the box on one side and a repeat of the cover of the booklet on the other.

In 2003, during the wide-scale remaster program applied to the band, *Bonfire* was reissued in a couple different digipak longbox formats, one with five disc trays and one with four that allowed the *Back in Black* disc its own independent package. Assuaging somewhat fans' complaints at the dearth of material included—the band countered the grumblings, saying they didn't have much in terms of Bon-era rarities—we'd soon see another box set, the *Backtracks* package from 2009, that offered a similar clutch of non-LP curios aided toward the comparatively substantive by the freedom to go beyond Bon into the Brian era.

36
ROCK THE BLUES AWAY:
FOURTEENTH ALBUM, STIFF UPPER LIP

It was Jon Anderson and his manager Sheryl Preston who discovered Bruce Fairbairn dead in his apartment, at the age of forty-nine, due to unknown causes—some have conjectured heart attack, others an aneurysm—after the famed producer failed to show up for a day of mixes on *The Ladder*, the eighteenth record from prog legends Yes.

Fairbairn was set to reprise his starring role played on AC/DC's *The Razors Edge*, the band hoping to score an impressive comeback in 2000 similar to the one experienced exactly ten years previous. Showing their respect, both Angus and Malcolm went to Fairbairn's funeral; and the band indeed set about working again in Vancouver, the beautiful coast Canadian city in which Fairbairn had delivered the 1990 hit record.

But instead of setting up shop at Little Mountain Studios, they picked The Warehouse, Bryan Adams's joint, bringing back elder Young brother George to produce and, notably, Fairbairn's right-hand man Mike Fraser to dial in the sounds. Fortunately, the record that the team would come up with doesn't sound like George's last kick at the can, the muddy and distorted *Blow Up Your Video*. But nor does it have the sharp elbows of *The Razors Edge*. If anything, *Stiff Upper Lip*, issued February 28, 2000, would sound like a slightly softened version of *Ballbreaker*, which was recorded in another world, Los Angeles, with Rick Rubin producing. There is arguably more Fraser to the surface sound of the album, but George was said to have been instrumental in keeping the sessions fun, keeping them rock 'n' roll and relaxed and, crucially, allowing Brian to sing in more comfortable ranges versus previous platters.

Writing went quickly, with Malcolm and Angus working together in the summer of 1997 and into February of 1998, in London and at Angus's home in the Netherlands, often with Angus on drums. The brothers also cooked up the lyrics, their concerns and their turns of phrases ringing somewhat like Brian and even Bon but somehow nerdier, more isolated, occasionally obscure and inscrutable.

Explains Fraser, "The direction they wanted to go in with *Stiff Upper Lip* . . . I think it was where they were trying to get to on *Ballbreaker* but didn't quite manage. But on this one they said, look, we're a blues band, we love the blues, we just want to get it all real tight. They didn't want any effects on it, or very little effects. Not that they're a very effect-y kind of band anyway, but they didn't want the big room sound on the drums. They wanted everything tight and in your face. So that's really the only thing we needed to discuss. You know, I've been a huge AC/DC fan forever, so for me it's pretty easy to say, 'Yeah, that sounds great' or 'That's not so good' [laughs]. I think that's why they got me to remaster all their back catalog. I knew what they wanted, and they didn't have to be there and they didn't have to approve it."

If *Ballbreaker* was the work of a band trying hard to shake off the rust of having been away—and *The Razors Edge* finding the guys working even harder, still at that point fully driven by competitive fires—*Stiff Upper Lip* was the work of a band on a victory lap, in no hurry to

This spread: At the National Exhibition Centre, Birmingham, U.K., November 28, 2000

impress, resulting in songs like "Can't Stand Still," "Hold Me Back," and "Meltdown," each of them down-home and positively boot-scuffin' an' line danceable, delicately sculpted and then stuck at the front half of the album. Soft contours from Angus add to the subtraction. His tone is clean, there's much palm-muting of his individually picked notes and chords, and he's mixed in judicious use of finger-picking, giving the riffs a sort of delicate embroidery. Malcolm is sympathetically conservative of tone and reticent about playing too hard, all of which can be heard unencumbered due to Phil Rudd's spare timekeeping.

For those who know their boogie rock, there's a parallel here to both Status Quo and Foghat going pop at the beginning of the 1980s yet somehow regularly still playing traditional rock 'n' roll, with performance and production and lighthearted melodies all conspiring to soften the end product. Indeed, one might call *Stiff Upper Lip* the *Powerage* of the Brian era, where the aggressive elbowing of other bounding bands is put aside for a strange and charming sense of being in the moment.

Still, there are singles that rustle up some level of taking care of business. The opening title track is by far the most famed song on the record and the most risible of both riff and rhythm. As for the concept, Angus was celebrating the great lips of rock 'n' roll, Elvis in full sneer, Mick just being Mick, and indeed himself on the cover of *Highway to Hell*. There's also Brian's lascivious look into his own pants, declaring "I was born with a stiff [pause, snort], stiff upper lip," set against a third layer of meaning, an expression of British stoicism, of not complaining and just getting on with it.

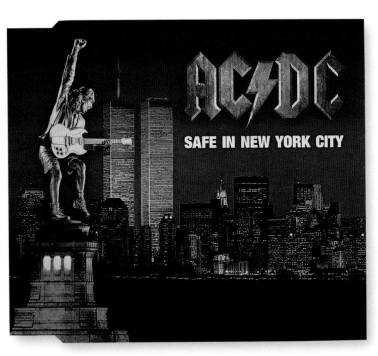

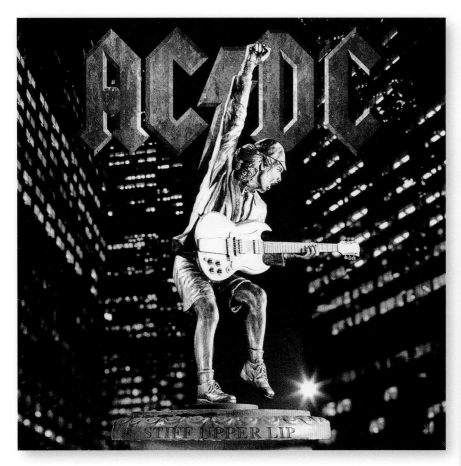

The fastest song on the record, "Safe in New York City," was also a single, the odd title (and nothing else about the lyric) arising from the sentiment that they were finding The Big Apple under Mayor Rudy Giuliani surprisingly safe, although at the end of the song, Brian says "I'd feel safe in a cage . . . Throw away the key." After the terrorist attacks of 2001, the song was included in the Clear Channel memo as a track deemed inappropriate for radio play. Further dismay comes from the fact that the cover art used for the single release featured the band's new prop, a bronze statue of Angus, planted right next to the twin towers of the World Trade Center.

Oddly, the video for the track featured the band playing in a blocked-off traffic tunnel (2nd Street Tunnel, Los Angeles), while "Stiff Upper Lip" had them busting out the song in Courtlandt Alley in Manhattan, after their red Hummer gets stuck in traffic. The swaggering and Stones-y "Satellite Blues" (Brian's favorite track on the record and his choice for single) was similarly shot in a sort of high-tech tunnel, resulting in all of the cinematic visuals for the album looking incongruously urban against the modest matchbox vibe of the songs and their sonic presentation this time out.

Stiff Upper Lip did modest business in the marketplace, reaching #7 on the Billboard charts and certifying platinum, a drop from *Ballbreaker* and short of the band's next record, *Black Ice*, as well. But from it we got a big bold Angus in bronze, not to mention a world tour that lasted pretty much an entire year, followed by one of the band's typical long stretches out of the spotlight, save for a clutch of appearances in 2003.

37
SHOOT TO THRILL:
AC/DC PERFORM ON *SNL*

It's one of those cultural milestone bucket-list items—doing *Saturday Night Live*—and AC/DC finally checked that one off by appearing on the nationally broadcast comedy show March 18, 2000, performing "Stiff Upper Lip" and "You Shook Me All Night Long."

The episode was hosted by wrestler Dwayne "The Rock" Johnson, and also featured here and there throughout are his World Wrestling Federation compatriots Triple H, Big Show, and Mick Foley, with boss Vince McMahon also appearing during the cold opening. It was season 25, episode 15, and it's an extremely well-done episode throughout, featuring lots of The Rock being impressively versatile, helped in the hitting of his marks by future stars like Will Ferrell and Jimmy Fallon.

Culturally speaking, Bill Clinton was president but there were references to George Bush and Al Gore fighting it out for who would be next. Chillingly, during Weekend Update with Colin Quinn, a joke about Osama bin Laden's kidney dialysis machine being powered by stationary bike was followed up with one about someone storming the cockpit of a passenger jet. Still, watching it again, I was reminded just how good this entire cast was in this era, with The Rock sending the night over the top and AC/DC being the hard rock icing on the cake.

"Stiff Upper Lip" came first, Brian all in black, charming as ever, singing up a storm, not missing a note. The whole band seemed to be having a blast, with a bespectacled Phil (in white T-shirt) throwing his shoulder into the big beat. Mal and Cliff augmented the performance with their typical grumbling old man backing vocals, and Angus peeled off a cracker of a guitar solo.

Anybody hoping for one of the guys to show up in a comedy sketch, however brief, would have been disappointed; for the next time we'd see the band is for their rendition of "You Shook Me All Night Long," played just a shade slow, all 'round somewhat tentatively, as if they had been simultaneously reminiscing about the long journey that had brought them to this place. Once again, Angus's hat flipped off at the start and Brian's stayed on, with Mal (gray tank top) and Cliff (white sneakers) once again stepping to their mics for a round of endearing rough mumbles. At the close, Angus collapsed to the floor for a wiggly worm guitar freak-out, after which he popped up and shut the song's door with a clang.

A few more quite funny "Rock"-solid sketches later and the show was over. During the traditional collective wave goodnight, Angus was on Triple H's shoulders with a wrestling belt draped over him. The Rock shook hands with the guys in the band, and Brian, all smiles, did a little jig. Thus concluded the single time AC/DC was ever on *Saturday Night Live*, fortunately bringing to the party the sturdy and starchy "Stiff Upper Lip," the best damn song they'd written since "Thunderstruck" and, before that, "Who Made Who."

Angus and Malcolm flank Jose Luis Perez, mayor of the Madrid district of Leganes, following the inauguration of a new street with the group`s name on March 22, 2000, just a few days after their *SNL* appearance.

38
SCHOOL DAYS:
AC/DC PLAY CLUB SHOWS AND SUPPORT THE ROLLING STONES

The *Stiff Upper Lip* campaign long over, AC/DC took 2002 off and then spent 2003 in a surreal space—or a number of spaces, as it were. It all began with Angus and Malcolm ambling on stage to perform a near-deconstructed version of B.B. King's "Rock Me Baby" with The Rolling Stones, who were in the middle of their *Forty Licks* tour. The surprise club gig took place at the 2,000-capacity Enmore Theatre in Sydney, on February 18, supported by local heroes Jet, a once-removed "baby AC/DC," with the most adjacent besides them being Airbourne (depending on where you rank The Angels, Rose Tattoo, and Heaven!).

Next came a club show of their own, ticketed but free, with AC/DC playing the Roseland Ballroom in New York on March 11, supported by Vendetta Red. This was the day after the band's Rock and Roll Hall of Fame induction, the subject of this book's next entry. The guys performed a full set that included deep *Powerage* tracks "Gone Shootin'" and "What's Next to the Moon." Notably missing was the "For Those About to Rock (We Salute You)" encore number. This was followed by another club show at the Columbiahalle in Berlin on June 9 featuring a similar but slightly longer set played under passing-out-hot conditions, with a notable addition to the sweaty dance card being "Bad Boy Boogie." Crowd size was pegged at around 3,000 with support coming from the all-girl Cyberspace Hippies.

Four days later, the guys returned to the old days as sandwich band, playing before The Rolling Stones and after The Cranberries in front of a crowd of 70,000 at the O-Vision Park in Oberhausen, Germany. It was a historic event, having AC/DC not headline; but there's no one else they could sensibly support, given their own stature at the top of the rock 'n' roll heap as well as their deep reverence for the Stones, who pretty much represented the biggest influence on AC/DC, clear in the music AC/DC would craft, which is essentially a heavy metal

Angus joins the Stones on stage at the Molson Canadian Rocks for Toronto festival, July 30, 2003.

version of the Stones, two steps past the Stones' own blues influences. Once again, up came Malcolm and Angus to help prop up the band's falling-down "Rock Me Baby."

Next came another club show, on June 17 at the Circus Krone in Munich, with AC/DC and the Cyberspace Hippies entertaining a crowd of about 2,500. Then it was back to sandwich band status—The Pretenders, AC/DC, Stones—at Festiese, Leipzig, Germany, June 20, playing to a crowd of 65,000, followed by one more show with the same bill in Hockenheim, Germany, two nights later, with AC/DC playing a shortened set distinguished by the presence of "Rock 'n' Roll Damnation" as the first encore selection.

A month would pass before the band's historic run with the Stones would come to an end, with the two blues rock giants headlining a benefit show in Toronto (more on that later). AC/DC would close out the second half of 2003 with only one more show, and to add to the strangeness that was the band's 2003, this one wouldn't be a club show or a big Stones-led affair. On October 21, AC/DC would play to a crowd of 5,000 to celebrate the opening of the Hammersmith Apollo, formerly the Hammersmith Odeon, which the band hadn't played in twenty-one years. Support would come from U.K. act Hundred Reasons,

who'd scored a bit of a hit with their 2002 debut album, *Ideas Above Our Station*. Tickets were priced at ten British pounds, which is what they would have been back in 1982.

To add to the surreal nature of AC/DC's year, the night before the official Hammersmith gig, the band performed a full lights and stage rehearsal version of the longer show to come, blasting their way through "If You Want Blood (You've Got It)," "Gone Shootin'," "Hard as a Rock," and "T.N.T." It's hard to picture a better four-song set for the deep fans, and that's what fifty contest winners, press people, and special guests experienced that night in October, witnessing what was the ultimate (or at least most intimate) AC/DC club show of 2003. And that was it. AC/DC's last three shows of the year would be in front of crowds of 500,000, fifty, and 5,000, after which five years would pass before they'd ever play live again.

A group photo including numerous artists who played the massive outdoor show in support of SARS relief at Downsview Park in Toronto.

39
ROCK THE HOUSE:
THE ROCK AND ROLL HALL OF FAME INDUCTION

Rock & Roll Hall of Fame 2003

Eighteenth Annual Induction Dinner
March 10, 2003

Across this tome of fifty career highlights (or, variously, milestones and goalposts), an induction into the Rock and Roll Hall of Fame would represent a traditional sort of apex achievement, that is, of course, depending on your tolerance for the place and the way it runs. To be sure, there have been vehement detractors or, at the mild end, those who downplay the existence of such awards in general; but AC/DC accepted the honor, bestowed upon them on March 10, 2003, with grace.

Joining them on the roster for the ceremonial night in New York were The Clash (inducted by The Edge and Tom Morello), Elvis Costello and the Attractions (inducted by Elton John), The Police (inducted by Gwen Stefani), and The Righteous Brothers, brought into the fold by Billy Joel. Ushering AC/DC in was the usual video montage and Aerosmith's Steven Tyler (inducted in 2001), whose speech was, ahem, colorful, with Tyler half vamping and half reading an adjective-laden description of the magic of AC/DC that reflected his personality and his true understanding and appreciation for the band. He even pulled out a crumpled note documenting a brief chat he had with Angus, proceeding to do a pretty good on-the-fly impression of Angus and his complicated accent.

Next up was Brian, who began by quoting a good chunk of "Let There Be Rock" in tribute to Bon, pointing out that Bon's nephews Paul and Daniel would be accepting the award on Bon's behalf. Amusingly, within a speech that barely ran a minute, the thank you list was short, as Brian name-checked Albert Music "for sticking with the boys" along with Atlantic, Elektra, "our new record company" Epic, and the fans "all around the world who have stuck by us through thick and thin."

On the night, the guys first played "Highway to Hell," with Angus wearing his tiny cap and lit devil horns and doing his guitar between Brian's legs bit for added effect. Then, after the break for the ceremony, Angus quipped, "We gotta sing for our supper;" and it was onto "You Shook Me All Night Long," the second and last song for the night. For this one, they were joined by Steven Tyler, who ambled on stage already singing at the end of the first verse, after which he proceeded to do a stellar job, hitting all the notes, establishing rapport with both Angus and Cliff, duetting his heart out with Brian, sometimes in unison and sometimes providing harmonies. It was jarring to see Tyler in sunglasses, a plain white dress shirt, and black pants, given his usual peacock attire—and boy, did he look tall.

Is it a slight that AC/DC were not inducted into the Hall of Fame until their third year of eligibility? Not really, because there's always a pile of acts to consider, as well as the fact that the institution had only begun its annual induction procedure in 1986. To be sure, the brief lag could also be chalked up to the notable anti-hard rock bias of the place, along with a slight skewing toward American acts. In any event, AC/DC were included relatively swiftly and have now been part of the brick and mortar of the Cleveland headquarters for twenty long years. Does it matter? That's up for fierce and usually quite nasty debate every year and twice a year, first when the fresh batch of nominees are announced and second when the actual inductees are picked. Credit where credit is due, the Rock and Roll Hall of Fame has found considerable traction while other music award institutions have faltered and weakened (most notably the Grammys) or gone out of business altogether. Bottom line, yea or nay, the Hall of Fame persists and AC/DC are more than deserving of their place in it.

Brian takes all the credit (while Angus says, "Wait a minute...") at the Rock and Roll Hall of Fame induction, New York City, March 10, 2003.

40
SKIES ON FIRE:
PERFORMING AT THE TORONTO ROCKS BENEFIT

Few folks remember this, but back in 2003, Toronto had for itself a small run-through of the worldwide COVID pandemic that hit the world hard beginning in March 2020. SARS, or severe acute respiratory syndrome, started in China in November 2002 and was traced to cave-dwelling bats. It was over by June 2003, with 8,469 cases reported worldwide and a fatality rate of 11 percent. Almost all the SARS cases were in the Far East, but 251 cases were logged in the province of Ontario and virtually all of them in the Toronto region. There were 43 deaths.

As a sort of pick-me-up for the city of Toronto, promoter Michael Cohl and The Rolling Stones—at the behest of a couple of Canadian politicians, Jerry Grafstein and Dennis Mills—devised the idea of a huge benefit concert in the form of an all-day festival that the Stones would headline. Of note, because of the virus, the World Health Organization had issued a travel advisory for Toronto, greatly reducing hotel bookings. It has been estimated that 100,000 hospitality jobs had been lost in the crisis. In addition, Canada had also recently dealt with an outbreak of mad cow disease. As for the involvement of Mick and Keith, the Stones have had a long history with Toronto,

playing small club shows there (most famously the El Mocambo) along with rehearsing in and around the city in preparation for tours.

In modern parlance, Molson Canadian Rocks for Toronto (more commonly known as Toronto Rocks or SARStock) might be called a super-spreader event; but again, the show took place at the tail end of the crisis on July 30, 2003, and outdoors on a beautiful summer day at Downsview Park, northwest of the city. Attendance was pegged at between 450,000 and half a million, making it the biggest ticketed event ever to take place in Canada.

The dance card for the eleven-hour event was themed heavily toward big Canadian stars past and present. Featured earlier in the day were Sam Roberts, La Chicane, Kathleen Edwards, Sass Jordan, The Tea Party, and Jeff Healey. Mid-day saw performances by Blue Rodeo and The Guess Who, with the headliners on the Canadian side of things being Rush, who played third from the top of the bill. An apprehensive Rush had been the last band booked, this being only the fourth (and last) time they'd ever done a festival gig. Also on the bill were the Have Love Will Travel Review (Dan Aykroyd and Jim Belushi), The Flaming Lips,

The Isley Brothers, and most controversially Justin Timberlake, who didn't go down well with the classic rock-oriented crowd, good sported as he was to entertain, knowing he was in enemy territory.

Essentially, however, the concert featured three headliners, beginning with Rush playing the first long-ish set of the night at eight songs, followed by AC/DC playing twelve songs, and then The Rolling Stones rocking and rolling through sixteen selections, with Angus and Malcolm joining the lads (as they'd done three times previously) for a rendition of "Rock Me Baby" deep into the night.

This wouldn't be the only time AC/DC would take the stage at a large outdoor event just as the sun was setting, but it might represent the most magical instance of that, given the size of the crowd, the charitable vibe of the show, and the fact that it was a perfectly hot but not scorching heart-of-summer day in Toronto that July 30.

It was surprising to hear the band open with "Hell Ain't a Bad Place to Be," but as Malcolm explained to me in our interview at the hotel the next day, "We didn't want to start off over-strong. We just wanted to creep into this, rather than a big she-bang. So we played a song that, like, probably only our die-hard fans know. And that sort of set us up, you know?"

Then we got "Back in Black," "Dirty Deeds Done Dirt Cheap," "Thunderstruck," "If You Want Blood (You've Got It)," "Hells Bells," "The Jack," "T.N.T.," "You Shook Me All Night Long," "Whole Lotta Rosie," "Let There Be Rock," and finally "Highway to Hell." It was widely reported by myself and others that AC/DC represented the highlight of the night, as once the Stones came on, there was a detectable sense of distraction in the crowd as sensible Canadians started wondering how the hell they were going to get out of the decommissioned military base grounds and back home again before morning.

But AC/DC had been to this kind of rodeo before. "The biggest show we've ever done was Moscow in, like, 1991," noted Malcolm. "That was when they got their democracy. It was like a week after Yeltsin and the tanks in the streets and the students. And a week later we were there playing. There were figures thrown around like one million people, and then the lowest figure was 600,000. No one knew exactly—it was Russia and they were counting from helicopters. I would say around 700,000. But that was a free show. We've done a couple of the gigs in Rio as well, to around 400,000.

"But it was good actually, because we were talking to the Stones and Keith says, 'We've never played in front of this many people.' And I was kind of like, really?! [laughs] So it was good—we were ready for it. But still, when you come out and have a look at that audience, you just go, 'How the hell are we going to get through to this?!' But I guess the sound relays and there are the big screens. I mean, at one point when we walked up, just everything was moving out there, right away, as far as you could see. It was just happening all the time, and it was certainly an experience for us. I think it meant a bit more here for the people, just to get everyone back into Toronto. And we tried our hardest. Yeah, we're not good with the politics and diseases and things [laughs], but we do know how to play and we just focused on that. And if it takes everything away for a while, for an hour, if people can just forget about everything else, even their bills at home, it's just a good thing, you know?"

This spread: Angus and Brian celebrate sundown at a huge decommissioned Canadian Forces base northwest of downtown Toronto.

41
ROCK AND ROLL AIN'T NOISE POLLUTION:
FIFTEENTH STUDIO ALBUM, *BLACK ICE*

Satan himself at the Allstate Arena, Chicago, October 30, 2008

Ending the longest gap between albums, *Black Ice*, AC/DC's fifteenth album, was issued on October 20, 2008, nearly nine years after the uncurling of *Stiff Upper Lip*. This was a different retail environment as well. AC/DC were one of the last holdouts with respect to selling their music as digital files or to streaming sites, and *Black Ice* was part of that era for the band, who went the novel route of selling only physical copies and, in North America, exclusively through Walmart.

And what did the punters get for their money? Well, they got the longest AC/DC album ever, *Black Ice* running nearly 56 minutes over fifteen tracks, each of typical AC/DC length, specifically 3:09 at the short end for the menacing, marauding "War Machine," and 4:41 at the long end for the unusually pensive and melancholy "Rock N Roll Dream."

Writing sessions conducted by Angus and Malcolm reached back to 2003 in London, but the real work would take place at The Warehouse in Vancouver, with Brendan O'Brien producing to no discernable effect. *Black Ice* sounds analog, polite, and perfect like the two that came before it, as well as the two that would come after, both similarly produced without edge by O'Brien.

Fortunately, good songs are plentiful, beginning with advance single "Rock N Roll Train," which finds the band in their Rolling Stones happy place. For classic rock fans, this was the song of the summer, seeing issue on August 28, 2008, creating substantial anticipation for a great album from the boys. Also issued as singles were the swaggering "Big Jack" as well as "Anything Goes," the latter being quite the departure for the band, a sort of Celtic-flavored pop song with a shockingly singsongy vocal melody out of Brian. The last single, into June 2009, was "Money Made," one of a clutch of southern rock-flavored songs on the album, with "Stormy May Day" going the furthest this way given Angus's use of slide guitar at O'Brien's behest.

Also at O'Brien's urging, the band was prompted to use material that was up-tempo and hooky, and then play it live as much as possible. "Spoilin' for a Fight," "Wheels," and "Rocking All the Way" definitely keep the party going but are also lean southern rock and Stones-y, less so awkward and bluesy as was the case on the last two "curious" records, and more barroom rocking, recalling the things people love about *Powerage*. O'Brien also pushed Brian as a singer, resulting in him only being able to work an hour a day.

Black Ice draws to a close with the heavy riffing of the title track, although now we're back to this vague complaint over presentation: If "Black Ice" or "Decibel" or indeed "Stiff Upper Lip" had been electrically mainlined into our veins like the bad-boy boogies from *Let There Be Rock*, *Powerage*, and *Flick of the Switch*, they'd be forever celebrated as late-period hoodlum rock anthems. But because of meticulous, fusspot performances and the safety net underneath the band's sound, beginning at *Ballbreaker*, no one talks about late-period AC/DC highlights, other than the songs we've had shoved down

our throats from a marketing standpoint, that is, usually the advance singles or things associated with video games or movies or sports. (Case in point: "War Machine" was linked with *Iron Man 2*, while "Spoilin' for a Fight" tag-teamed with World Wrestling Entertainment).

Black Ice, through the band's new deal with Sony, was issued as a digipak with either red, white, or yellow lettering used for the logo, as well as a deluxe hardcover edition and an ultra-deluxe metal box edition and double vinyl. Walmart rolled out the red carpet and created for the album's presentation over 3,000 "Rock Again AC/DC Stores," which included as part of the display other AC/DC albums, the *No Bull* live DVD, the *AC/DC Live: Rock Band* video game, as well as the band's clothing line.

It's no surprise that a mere month after the album's issue, *Black Ice* was simultaneously certified gold, platinum, and double platinum for sales of over two million copies, with an estimated six million copies of the album shifted worldwide by the end of 2008. The long wait and attendant impressive full-court press marketing campaign surely had something to do with the album's success, but so did the lively material all over the album itself, with *Black Ice* arguably ranking as the band's best album since *The Razors Edge* all the way back in 1990. Also surely helping was the massive year-and-a-half tour in support of the album (representing the band's first extensive slew of dates since 2001), with the guys rocking their way through five songs from the new record while dwarfed by an onstage locomotive weighing in at 3500 kg (nearly four tons!).

At the Wachovia Arena in Wilkes-Barre, Pennsylvania, October 28, 2008

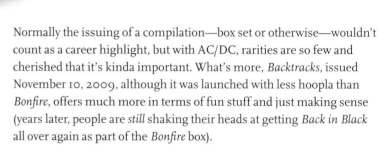

42

BOOGIE MAN:

COLUMBIA ISSUES *BACKTRACKS* BOX SET

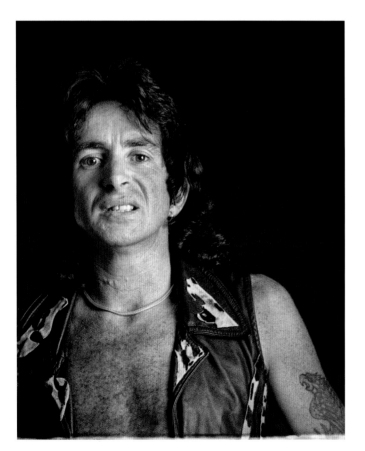

Normally the issuing of a compilation—box set or otherwise—wouldn't count as a career highlight, but with AC/DC, rarities are so few and cherished that it's kinda important. What's more, *Backtracks*, issued November 10, 2009, although it was launched with less hoopla than *Bonfire*, offers much more in terms of fun stuff and just making sense (years later, people are *still* shaking their heads at getting *Back in Black* all over again as part of the *Bonfire* box).

Even the live material here has a more studied sense of curation, with the tracks not being random but sort of historic and official, originating as B-sides of 7" and 12" singles and the like. And it's all essentially a couple and done and onto the next track, with no lazy banks and chunks of concerts, the bonus being that the origin story of each track is meticulously sorted for us without the usual obscuring we tend to get from big bands. Highlights for the deep fan include "Shot Down in Flames" from the Hammersmith Odeon in 1979, an absolutely blazing "Guns for Hire" from Detroit in 1983, and "This House Is on Fire" from that same Detroit show, even if on this one, Brian is fighting for his life. Then there's "Safe in New York City," tight, urgent, recorded in Phoenix in 2000, this time the whole band fighting for their lives and winning the struggle, rocking out hard, especially when Angus tears into his cantankerous solo. Finally, there's a sampling of the insanity of the monumental Moscow gig with what are arguably the headiest songs of any AC/DC show (and both for different reasons along a rainbow of emotions), namely "Highway to Hell" and "For Those About to Rock (We Salute You)."

The included DVD, essentially an extension of the *Family Jewels* video package from 2005, delivers all those classic production videos, young and old, along with the making of "Hard as a Rock" and the making of "Rock N Roll Train" segments. I dunno, DVDs always muddy the waters of these things, but there you go: *Backtracks* is now a multimedia package, augmented further by a thirty-six-page booklet comprised mostly of pictures, because what more is there to say?

I must point out at this point that there's a deluxe version of *Backtracks* and a standard version and that all tracks on both are remastered. The deluxe features a bunch of packaging accoutrements plus about 50 percent more rarities and 100 percent more live tracks. We're sticking with the standard here, to be as everyman as possible, just like Angus or Mal when you get them talking.

And so over to the studio rarities, there are twelve tracks here, versus the eighteen you get with the deluxe. But don't you worry, all the key stuff is here, with, frankly, the additional six ringing superfluous. The early-days Bon-era essentials are "Stick Around," "Carry Me Home" (chilling, when you think of how Bon died), "Crabsody in Blue," and most pertinently *Powerage*-era classic "Cold Hearted Man," a desperado barnstormer that sounds like the front cover of Motörhead's *Ace of Spades*. Also included are "Love Song," "Fling Thing," and "R.I.P. (Rock in Peace)," all of them not deemed worthy by Atlantic for American consumption for a reason.

Then there's a shift to the shiny 1980s, where we find out the band was busy with non-LP songs concocted for various reasons. Unfortunately, neither "Snake Eye," "Borrowed Time," nor "Down on the Borderline" are much more than phoned-in hair metal crossed with *Fly on the Wall* purposelessness. Upmarket, however, is the chunky "Big Gun," fired off for the *Last Action Hero* soundtrack. Equally aggressive and military-grade is "Cyberspace," an uptempo rocker doomed to ring dated but nonetheless effusive of riff and rhythm.

Again, it seems like *Backtracks* was put together with the best intentions in mind, namely to catch up on all the bits and pieces missed on *Bonfire*, which, granted, was trying to stick to the storyline that it was a celebration of the early days. Consider it mission accomplished, even if a dozen years later we now know there are many additional AC/DC songs in demo form that would be cool to hear and have documented on an official release.

Still, whether it's the Bon-era stuff or songs of dubious motivation with Brian, we learn through osmosis, by demonstration, that all the months and years of fretting Mal and Angus went through over what to put on the records . . . it was worth doing; it paid off. In other words, we're thankful to get the couple records' worth of studio things given to us in *Bonfire* and *Backtracks*, but we emerge from the experience in agreement with the guys that the studio albums as presented were the right way to go.

This spread: Looking back, AC/DC circa 1976

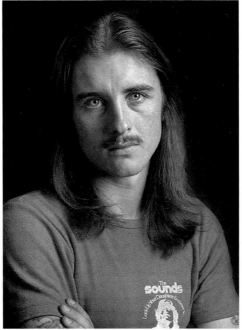

43

JAILBREAK:
A THIRD LIVE ALBUM, *LIVE AT RIVER PLATE*

The band at the film premiere of *Live at River Plate*, May 5, 2011, at the Hammersmith Apollo in London.

Live at River Plate serves as an AC/DC career highlight for the following poignant reason: It would be the last red-carpet filming, documentation, and official release from the classic *Back in Black* lineup live in all its glory. Malcolm would play his last concert with the band seven months later, and for additional resonance (if any was needed), the idea of Phil Rudd in the band moving forward past this point remains anyone's guess.

Essentially, this is AC/DC's version of Iron Maiden's *Rock in Rio* or Rush's *Rush in Rio*, namely a triumphant live stand in South America properly planned and recorded, representing a victory lap for the band at hand and indeed classic hard rock 'n' roll in general, given the party that all three sets turned into. As evidenced by the Rush and Iron Maiden albums and videos (as well as the Iron Maiden movie *Flight 666*), a South American heavy metal crowd is a beautiful thing, surging and ebbing like a roiling ocean, roaring along to the lyrics, banners flying, tears flowing.

The present situation had AC/DC playing at the stadium named (somewhat colloquially) for the Argentinean football club, River Plate, in Buenos Aires,

LIVE AT RIVER PLATE

over three sold-out nights to a total of 200,000 fans, on December 2, 4, and 6 of 2009. This was the band's first visit to Argentina since playing two nights at the same venue in October 1996. The present stand took place two-thirds the way through the immense tour campaign for the long-awaited *Black Ice* album, with the band setting up shop in Argentina after shows in San Juan, Puerto Rico, and São Paulo, Brazil, with planned dates in Lima, Peru, and Santiago, Chile, having to be scrapped.

AC/DC brought their full stage show, including bells and cannons and the immense locomotive centerpiece (ridden amusingly by the Rosie blow-up as she tapped her foot along to the uncommonly slowed-down version of "Whole Lotta Rosie") plus a long ramp that took Brian regularly into the middle of the teeming masses.

The set list for the production was extremely safe, stacked high with the hits, although "Hell Ain't a Bad Place to Be," "Dog Eat Dog," and "The Jack" represented somewhat the deeper reaches of the catalog. Most of value for freshness was "Rock N Roll Train," which opened the show after an extensive video segment featuring an excellent animated train narrative put together by Murray John (offered also as bonus material on the DVD). Most obscure, however, given that they were also from the new album, were "Big Jack," "War Machine," and most shockingly, the title track, "Black Ice," a gem from the 2008 record buried at the end of that album's long running order.

The shows were shot in high definition using thirty-two cameras and then deftly directed and edited by longtime AC/DC associate David Mallet for final consumption. The sound is so good it loses some of its live vibe, but then a ruff 'n' ready Brian, his vocal cords worn to bloody nubs after more than a year on the road, serves as a constant

reminder that what we are hearing is AC/DC on stage. Indeed the *Black Ice* tour was one of the biggest in the band's history, touching down in 128 cities across 28 countries, with the guys playing to an estimated five million fans.

The first issue of *Live at River Plate* was on May 10, 2011, as a DVD and Blu-Ray, with the double album CD issue, containing the same 19 tracks, arriving on November 19, 2012. The CD issue was in conjunction with the announcement that the band's catalog will finally be made available for digital purchase through iTunes—one might call this an attendant career highlight, with the band on that day selling 48,000 album downloads and 696,000 individual songs. AC/DC finally went digital long after the arrival of Spotify (founded in 2006 with a sort of staggered launch), following other famous holdouts like Metallica (2006), Led Zeppelin (2007), and, most famously for complaints, The Beatles in 2010. The news about AC/DC reluctantly embracing modern technology overshadowed the CD release of the album, which, granted, had already been out a year as a DVD and indeed featured an inferior album cover in audio format. Over the years, however, as discussed previously, *Live at River Plate* would take on added tragic resonance, first through the retirement of Malcolm as touring guitarist, then with his dementia diagnosis and finally his death.

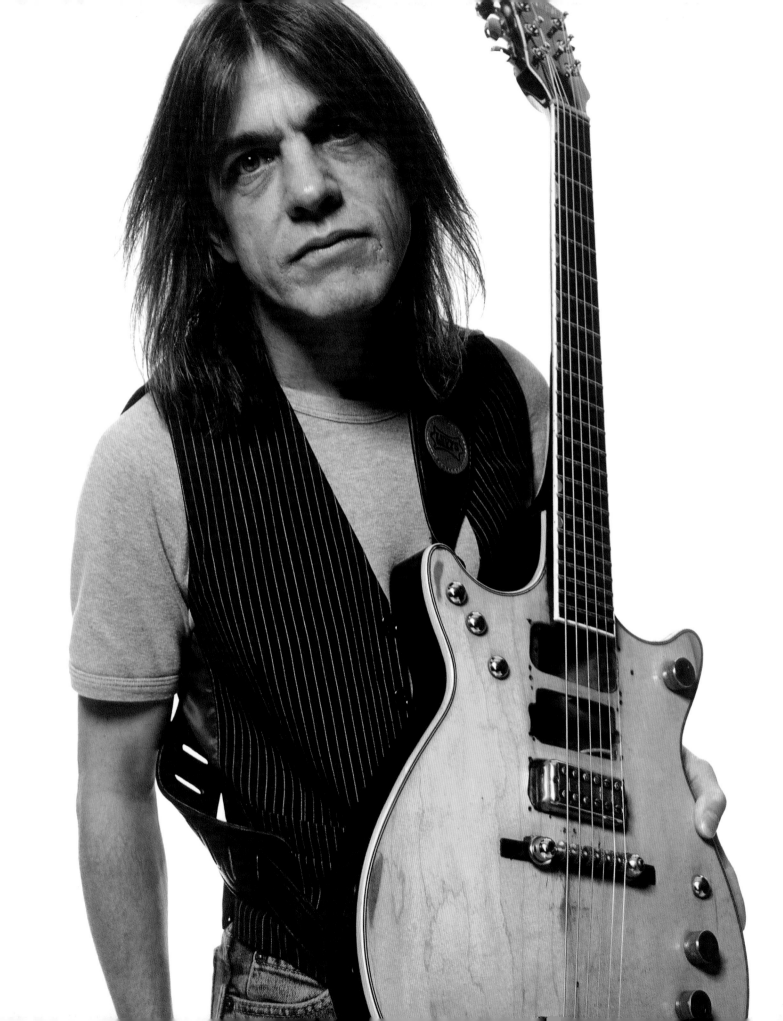

PART 4
MALCOLM

Malcolm Young, New
York City, March 2000

44

REALIZE:

ILL HEALTH FORCES MALCOLM ASIDE; PHIL RUDD GETS FIRED

As it turned out, Bon Scott wasn't the only one who wasn't indestructible.

All the chain-smoking and boozing these guys did finally caught up with Malcolm, who, after getting off the road at the end of the *Black Ice* tour, had to go under the knife for lung cancer, having been fitted for a pacemaker as well. On top of all this, according to interviews conducted by Angus, all the way back to the assembly of the *Black Ice* album in the spring of 2008, Malcolm's memory had been slipping. Once on the road, he had given in to treatment for it and would routinely rehearse the set before each show to make sure he could get through the night without mistakes.

Then came the announcements: On April 16, 2014, just before the band was gearing up to record a new album, AC/DC released a statement saying that Malcolm would be "taking a break from the band due to ill health." In May the band would be in Vancouver without Mal, with Brian revealing in July that the elder statesman of the band was, in fact, in the hospital. A leak came on September 26, with the report of a dementia diagnosis, prompting the family to follow up with a confirmation four days later.

Malcolm performing at a stadium colloquially known as The Ahoy, in Rotterdam, The Netherlands, during the *Black Ice* tour, March 13, 2009.

Malcolm's replacement—
and nephew—Stevie
Young, performing in
Roskilde, Denmark, July
15, 2015.

Malcolm would not play on the album, nor would he play with AC/DC live ever again. This renders the band's show at the Estadio San Mamés in Bilbao, Spain, to a crowd of 37,000 on June 28, 2010, as Malcolm's last concert with the band. Otherwise uneventful, and with a typical set list from the tour, the Bilbao show comes at the end of nearly two years on the road in support of *Black Ice*, with the campaign being the first full-press onslaught for the band since 2001.

Adding further significance to the show in Spain, that might have been the last time Phil drums for AC/DC ever again. There's been one tour since, and replacing Phil was Chris Slade. Of note, the first show with Chris took place on April 10, 2015, at Coachella in Indio, California, with this show also going into the history books as the first without Malcolm.

So where was Phil? Well, his problems began right after the *Black Ice* dates. First, on December 1, 2010, he was busted for possession of marijuana, which was found on his boat. Next he had a restaurant open and close and then reopen again, marbled with more legal issues, in which Phil was ordered to pay sizeable restitution based on the illegal firing of three employees. On November 14, 2014, after a raid on his home, he was charged with possession of cannabis and methamphetamine, along with attempting to procure a murder. The hit man charge was dropped the following day, but the other two stuck. This

was all happening five months after he'd completed work on the *Rock or Bust* album and, in fact, two weeks before the record was to be released, throwing the ensuing tour into question and otherwise tarnishing the band's good name, notwithstanding the tragic news we'd all been processing about Mal.

Five days after Chris played his first show with the band since the glory days supporting *The Razors Edge*, Phil pled guilty to the drug charges. On July 9, 2015, he was sentenced to eight months of home detention and fined $120,000 in New Zealand dollars. Two appeals to have his convictions overturned have been dismissed. As he told me a year later, after returning to drumming and even issuing a solo album called *Head Job*, "You better believe it, mate, I'm dangerous. I'm more dangerous than I've ever been before. I've sorted all my bullshit out, and my substance issues are all a thing of the past, and yeah, now I feel like a young fellow. I work out, but I sort of prefer to work out on the kit, you know? I don't really have any inherent or inside talents or capabilities. I just sort of swing at them and see what happens. Everyone sort of considers me to be the engine room of the band. The rhythm section is sort of nailed down by me. That's probably what I do best. I just nail it down, brother. I just keep it nailed down. The kids keep saying I'm making too much noise downstairs, but that's all right [laughs]."

45

PLAY BALL:

AC/DC ISSUE *ROCK OR BUST,* THEIR FIRST ALBUM WITHOUT MALCOLM

Amid the sad news about Malcolm and the scandalous news about Phil, AC/DC gamely said, "Let's play ball," issuing an advance single on October 7, 2014, that bode more than well for the soon-arriving *Rock or Bust* album. The song was in fact heard first on September 27 in a themed arrangement with Major League Baseball as the league geared up for the post-season and the World Series to follow in November. "Play Ball" was as happy, heady, and inviting as "Rock N Roll Train" was from the last album, and suddenly all eyes and ears were on AC/DC once again six years after the release of the last record from this part-time band.

Malcolm would not play on the album, with his relative and replacement from back in the 1980s, Stevie Young, joining the team full-time. The artful booklet for the album, featuring swanky black-and-white photos of the band, would pay tribute to AC/DC's fallen leader with a simple missive stating, "And most of important of all, thanks to Mal, who made it all possible." But it didn't stop there: Sticking with recent tradition, the credits for all the songs would go to Malcolm and Angus, with Angus quite rightly reminding us that the guys have always had tons of riffs and ideas carried over into the next set of sessions for years, adding that Malcolm would be considerably organized in recording and documenting them, making them easy to access. Back to the booklet, Phil isn't in some of the pictures because he arrived in Vancouver ten days

Jahnwiesen, Köln, Germany, June 19, 2015

Outside the *Rock or Bust* listening party at Webster Hall, New York City, November 18, 2014.

late for the sessions and almost got replaced, showing up just in the nick of time before O'Brien pulled the plug on him.

Other than the forced personnel change on account of Malcolm's condition, the band would go for comfort, recording once again with the Brendan O'Brien and Mike Fraser team at The Warehouse in Vancouver, laying down tracks starting on May 3, 2014, and finishing up July 14. Unfortunately, perhaps taking to heart complaints that *Black Ice* was too long or rife with filler or "a bit of a slog," the guys opted for the shortest album of their career, with *Rock or Bust*, issued on November 28, coming in at eleven songs and thirty-five minutes, which is a couple minutes shorter than second place, namely *Flick of the Switch* from back in 1983.

In this writer's opinion, *Black Ice* is a substantial creative triumph, but *Rock or Bust*, not so much, hampered by too many stodgy, geometric, blues-based riffs and chord progressions, awkward lyrics, and a recording that comes off as hot, sort of artificially distorted at the rhythm guitar end and similarly too distracted and sizzly at the high-hat, which Phil usually leaves fairly open and O'Brien leaves fairly high in the mix. But back to the writing, there's an almost-embarrassing ambling quality to things like "Dogs of War" and "Got Some Rock & Roll Thunder" (as you can see, AC/DC never decided on a consistent way to spell rock 'n' roll, despite sticking it in so many of their titles), as well as "Hard Times," that makes me think of new country and line dancing.

At the positive end, "Play Ball" is a happy-making anthem for the ages, with a non-obvious, obscure verse riff to boot, while "Baptism of Fire" is a welcome, menacing, late-period heavy metal rocker from the band. Tucked at the end of the album, "Sweet Candy" offers a bit of the ol' *Fly on the Wall* contact buzz, while closing track "Emission Control" is ambitious-of-riff construct, funky but also considerably heavy, representing a success of the earth-toned writing that elsewhere on the album stays unremarkably brown.

Issued as the second single from the album was the opening title track, a song that, in this writer's opinion, is saddled with most of the negatives mentioned previously, most pointedly its lyrics, which read like English as a second language Scorpions. Next for promotion was "Rockin' the Blues Away," another ill-advised choice due to its overly poppy melody reminiscent of the most singsongy track on the last album, namely "Anything Goes."

Still, the album was not particularly savaged by the critics and managed a #3 debut on the main Billboard charts and a #1 placement in Canada, always a good territory for AC/DC. *Rock or Bust* also quite quickly went gold, a certification level that was getting harder to reach with the steep decline in physical record sales well established by 2015, with the album also quite quickly amassing sales of 2.8 million copies worldwide. Soon, however, adding to the issues concerning Malcolm and Phil, the tenures of both Brian and Cliff within the ranks of AC/DC would soon come into question, leaving many to ponder whether the future of the band would be less rock and more bust.

46
NICK OF TIME:
PERFORMING AT THE GRAMMYS

It started painful, but—stay with me—it eventually got better. LL Cool J tried to sound excited but instead spewed some patronizing nonsense in his introduction to AC/DC performing live on the Grammy Awards for the first time ever. And then there they were. Like a Foo Fighters or a Metallica (set your watch), AC/DC were squirming on stage trying valiantly to remind people about learning instruments, darkly lit in the Staples Center on February 8, 2015, at the 57th Annual Grammy Awards. The song that Columbia and self-respect required them to play was "Rock or Bust," but it went over like a lead balloon because the song's basically a bad math class instead of prom night. No marauding camera cameos could find any of the pop glitterati enjoying themselves despite their bad acting.

But then came a second song from one of one of the world's greatest blues bands of all time, Brian and Angus delivering (albeit weirdly down-tempo) the rock 'n' roll damnation saga depicted in "Highway to Hell." Now we had a win. As metaphor for the difference between the two title tracks, separated by forty years and therefore approximately eight music-business generations, the ebullient and redeeming second performance revealed pure joy across the faces of the assembled jewelry-rattlers suddenly in touch with their rebellious youths.

As alluded to, I'm a case of "Who cares about the Grammys?," although I'm not as cynical as most about the Rock and Roll Hall of Fame. The Grammy Awards was enemy territory for AC/DC, but across the years it hadn't in fact been a complete spurning. *Blow Up Your Video* was nominated for the inaugural Best Hard Rock/Metal performance in 1989, following up with nominations for *The Razors Edge* in 1991, "Moneytalks" in 1992, and "Highway to Hell" (live) in 1994. Further betraying

typical Grammy fudging of timelines, 2009 saw AC/DC garnering a nomination for "Rock N Roll Train" in the Best Performance by a Duo or Group with Vocal category (are you gathering how dumb the Grammys are?). This was followed by an actual win in 2010 for "War Machine" in the Best Hard Rock Performance category and also a nomination for *Black Ice* in that year for Best Rock Album.

Additionally on the hardware front, there would be three Billboard Music Awards nominations, an American Music Awards nomination, and then the logical slew of nominations and wins for Australian ceremonies like the APRA Awards and the ARIA Awards. With respect to the somewhat-weighty MTV Video Music Awards, AC/DC would be nominated once, in 1991 for "Thunderstruck" in the Best Heavy Metal/Hard Rock Video category. The band lost out to "The Other Side" from Aerosmith, another 1970s band that managed to revive its career by going to Vancouver and working with Bruce Fairbairn.

Zoom forward to February 2015, on this Grammy night they indeed would be spurned like so many times before, on all those occasions when they'd been nominated just to keep the label brass happy. To be sure, the band was not up for any awards at the 57th annual soiree, but in reality, it was even more meaningful than that. AC/DC were playing live in tribute to Malcolm, who surely was on the minds of the industry insider attendees that night the same way they thought about their parents, experiencing the slow dark smothering of either dementia or Alzheimer's or at least ready candidates for either affliction. Feeling wistful, they watched Stevie Young instead of Mal and Chris Slade instead of Phil, representing the sunsetting—or doomed to be brief and uneventful next phasing—that is the destiny of a band getting old.

AC/DC SOUND-ALIKES

The AC/DC sound wasn't entirely original. Malcolm and Angus would tell you that it all comes from Chuck Berry and The Rolling Stones, but fact is, there's an element of the hard end of U.K. glam in it, as well as a bit of Stevie Wright and at least inspiration from the first heavier bands ever out of Australia like Billy Thorpe & the Aztecs, Buffalo, and Coloured Balls.

But this isn't about what came before, but rather the cottage industry in the AC/DC sound that emerged after the success of the heroes of our story. It begins in Australia, most pointedly with fellow Albert Productions act, The Angels. The first album is a bit of a wobbler, but 1978's *Face to Face*, 1979's *No Exit*, and 1980's *Dark Room* are classics, very much in the AC/DC vein but with a literary bent to the lyrics of Doc Neeson, now sadly no longer with us, having died from a brain tumour in 2014.

Next came Angry Anderson and Rose Tattoo, who found success with a bit of a rough and punky AC/DC-derived sound across the likes of the band's 1978 self-titled, *Assault & Battery* from 1981 and *Scarred for Life* from 1982. Then there's Heaven, with *Twilight of Mischief*, *Where Angels Fear to Tread*, and *Knockin' on Heaven's Door*. Alan Fryer and crew—Alan is also no longer with us, having passed from cancer in 2015—scored a bit of a novelty hit with "In the Beginning," which, like "Let There Be Rock,"

tells the story of rock 'n' roll while also featuring a few guitar licks from the history books. Flash forward and it's Jet, Airbourne, and The Lazys that uphold AC/DC's legacy on home turf.

Leaving down under, there was enough influence on French bands during the time of the adjacent New Wave of British Heavy Metal that the entire scene got characterized as biker rock with more than a hint of AC/DC heard across numerous bands, including Warning and Trust (and also Baron Rojo, from Spain). Up into the hair metal era we got Jackyl from Atlanta, who even did a duet with Brian Johnson on their *Cut the Crap* album called "Locked & Loaded." There was also Johnny Crash, D-A-D (from Denmark), and most notably Rhino Bucket, who, through records like 1992's *Get Used to It*, seemed to be intentionally aiming at the prize for most authentically imitative. Most commercially, perhaps, is the case of the Rick Rubin-produced *Electric* album by The Cult, even if for all intents and purposes the strong AC/DC influence proved to be more of a one-off.

But most famously adjacent was—and still is—Krokus, Switzerland's most famous rock 'n' roll export, in operation since 1975 but seriously AC/DC-like beginning with 1980's *Metal Rendez-Vous*. The two bands even shared live production companies and a producer in Tony Platt, and vocalist Marc Storace was one of the names put forward to replace Bon Scott when he died. Storace also says that Krokus were about to use cannons before AC/DC took up the idea circa *For Those About to Rock*. The influence would ebb and flow through the ensuing decades, but on 1981's *Hardware* and 1982's *One Vice at a Time*, the resemblance is uncanny. In fact, save for a cover of The Guess Who's "American Woman" on *One Vice at a Time*, there's barely a moment on the record that couldn't have dovetailed seamlessly into the likes of *Flick of the Switch* or *Fly on the Wall*.

Talk to the guys about it (as I have on many occasions), and without ire or irony they'd tell you that when they first heard AC/DC they fell in love with the sound, but also that the two bands' influences would have been similar. Still, Storace has also opined that there's something within the character of the Swiss and the French that draws them to this distinctive sound, hence an added validity to my comment earlier about the French bands of the early '80s. Whatever it is, when Krokus are on a tear—and the pinnacle of that would be "Long Stick Goes Boom"—they more than match the magic of the masters.

dead forever...
BUFFALO

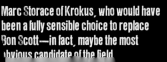

Marc Storace of Krokus, who would have been a fully sensible choice to replace Bon Scott—in fact, maybe the most obvious candidate of the field.

47

HELLS BELLS

BRIAN PLAYS HIS LAST AC/DC SHOW... TO DATE

It was just a typical Midwest arena show, but there's a good chance it's going to go down in history as the last concert Brian Johnson ever performs with AC/DC. After playing the Sprint Center in Kansas City, Missouri, on February 28, 2016—the show had already been moved a day to accommodate the funeral of a friend of Brian's—Johnson issued a statement that he was dealing with hearing problems and couldn't disappoint the fans and the band any longer.

According to Johnson, this all began eight years earlier, when he started experiencing deafness which he claims was due to his love of auto racing more than his job fronting AC/DC. He recalls racing at Watkins Glen and forgetting to put in his earplugs and then feeling a little pop in his ear which caused him six or seven months of tinnitus. He also talks about a cold outdoor show in Winnipeg where he caught a bad infection that caused him further issues, including crystallized fluid that, in his words, ate away at his ear.

For a singer, advanced deafness means you can't properly hear the rest of the band—the notes they're playing, the keys, or as Brian frames it, "the guitars"—with Cliff Williams remarking that he'd see Brian tear out his in-ear monitors in frustration, indicating that nothing was helping him connect to what the rest of the guys were doing. AC/DC would play another twenty-three shows on the *Rock or Bust* tour, comprising a European leg and American leg, with Axl Rose subbing for Brian.

Brian hooked up with cutting-edge hearing-aid specialist Stephen Ambrose, who brought along to the amiable Geordie an invention called ADEL. Brian was reticent to talk about it because he didn't want to give away the developing technology, but he did say that it was a big machine that together they were going to work to miniaturize, with the approach involving the use of the bone structure in the head as a sort of receiver. Johnson explained later with a chuckle that they worked two-and-a-half years together on perfecting the technology, calling the process "boring as shit."

Bottom line is that Brian said it was working, and so far, completely unexpected, there was a brand-new full-length studio album with Brian in 2020, called *Power Up*. And before that, Brian even guested at a show with Robert Plant and Paul Rodgers, howling away like a kid again. It all bodes well because let's not forget that this isn't the story of an old hard rocker with seized-up vocal cords, although screaming like that, Brian's never had it easy and there definitely has been some degradation. Fundamentally, this was a problem with the connection between what Brian needed to hear through his ears and what was going to come out of his mouth.

Of course, as a cruel twist of fate, just as he might have been ready to road-test Ambrose's new technology, the coronavirus pandemic hit, scotching everybody's touring plans. In the meantime, Brian was philosophical about the situation, remarking that he's had a "pretty good run" being part of "one of the best bands in the world."

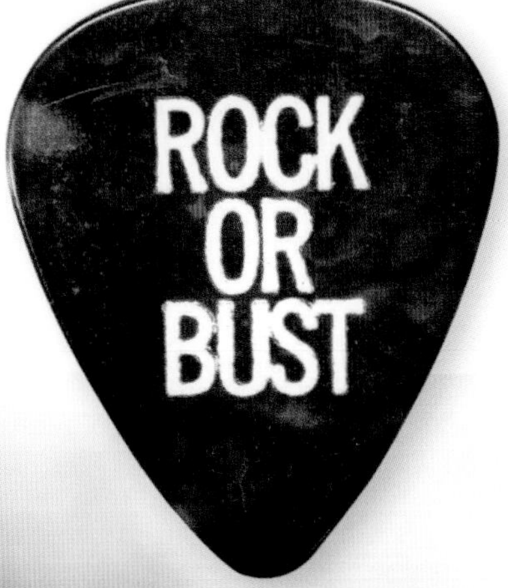

Sprint Center, Kansas City, Missouri, February 28, 2016

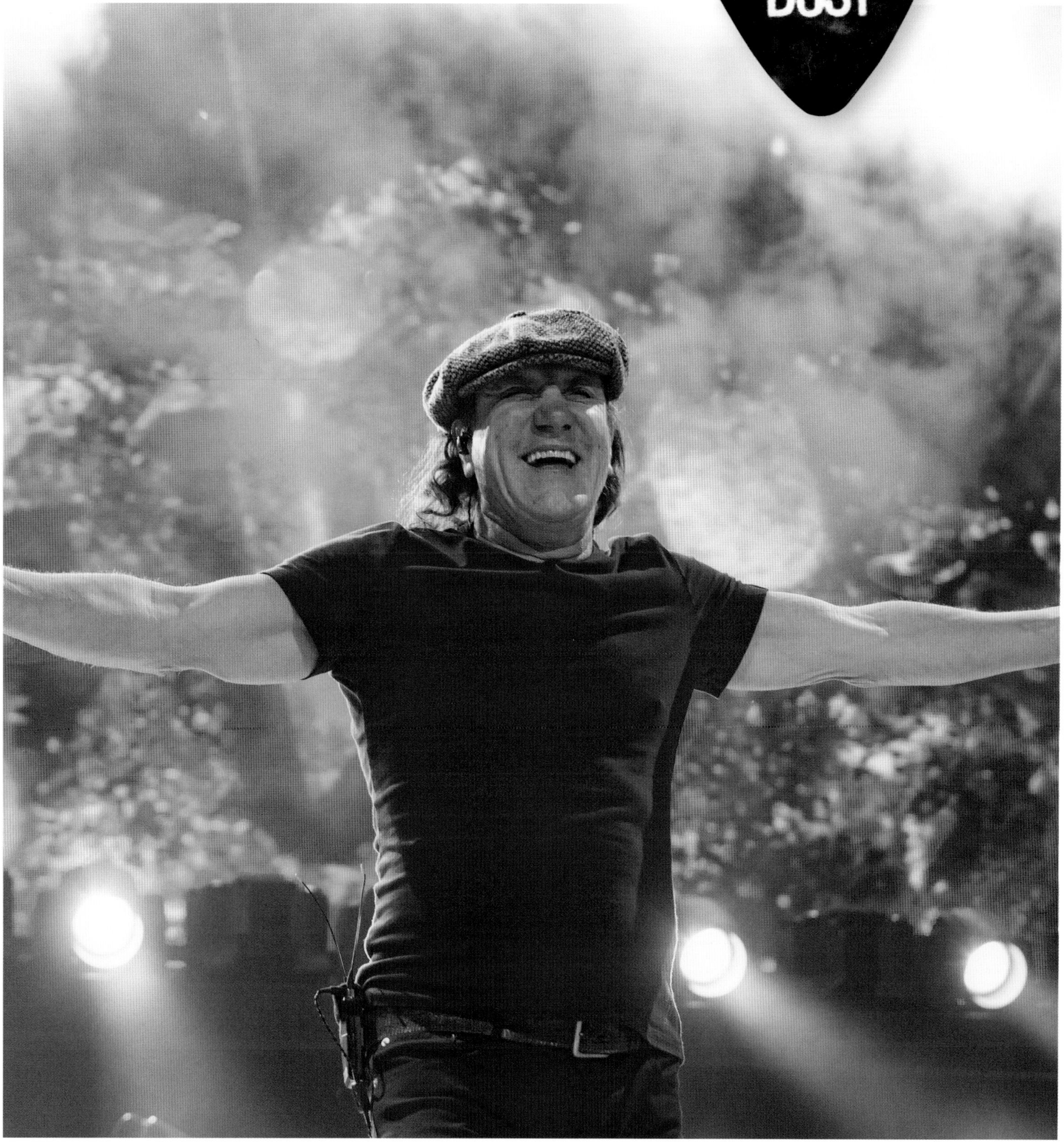

48

GUNS FOR HIRE:

TWENTY-THREE DATES WITH AXL ROSE AS FRONT MAN

On September 25, 1985, Eddie Van Halen jumped on stage with the Sammy Hagar band at Farm Aid; and it was soon known that the Red Rocker was joining the mighty Van Halen. Much the same happened on April 16, 2016, when Angus joined Guns N' Roses on stage at Coachella, with the announcement getting made that day that Axl was going to help AC/DC fulfill their tour commitments, standing in for Brian Johnson, who, it seemed, was being forced to quit the business due to his severe hearing-loss issues. Angus was resplendent in his powder-blue schoolboy outfit, including matching hat, as the band worked their way through "Whole Lotta Rosie." The crowd, of course, loved it, as did the Gunners, who grew up dreaming about the day they could conquer the world rocking the way AC/DC did back in 1981.

Of course the built-in betrayal of the Van Halen situation wasn't present here, with the Guns guys giving Axl their full blessing to take on this historic run of shows, confident in the fact that by no means was Axl leaving the Gunners to do the gig.

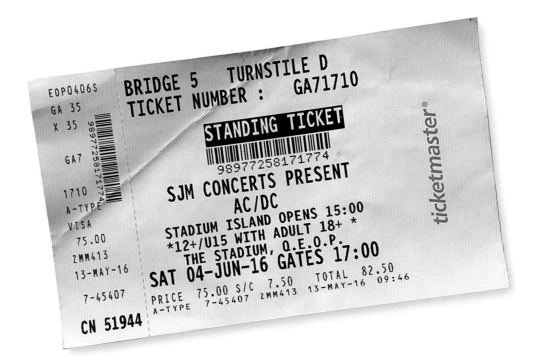

Auburn Hills, Michigan, *Rock or Bust* tour, September 9, 2016

The first thirteen shows were over in Europe, and things got off to a wobbly start. Axl had broken his foot and had been singing from a sort of throne on recent Guns shows, and he had to continue through this somewhat-comical situation for the first five shows in Europe, namely Lisbon, Seville, Marseilles, Paris, and Wechter, Belgium.

By May 19, in Vienna, he was up and at 'em, roaming the stage, indeed commanding it as he does, and all was right with the world again. Reports from fans and critics were effusive. Axl was respectful of both the band and the fans, working hard, hitting the high notes, and basically singing powerfully and dependably. It was a dream gig, and he knew it and, in fact, was so bold as to offer his services rather than wait to be asked by the band (fortunately, they said yes). As for interesting set list wrinkles, new since 1996 was "Riff Raff" and since 2003, "Rock 'n' Roll Damnation," both from 1978's *Powerage*, an AC/DC album regularly cited as a favorite by many a deep AC/DC fan.

But what of Axl Rose as a pick to play this role? Frankly, it felt both wrong and right. At the wrong end, Axl had been a guy that emitted bad vibes, although he had been much better behaved as of late. Second, he was American, in fact, the first-ever American in the band—and (essentially) from Los Angeles to boot, not an AC/DC kind of place. Third, he's got a high and thin voice, definitely quite different from the lascivious mongrel growl that both Bon and Brian had been dealing in. Finally, Axl's personality and presence is of such a stature that there was a sort of distracting factor to this all-too-gleaming teaming. I mean, mathematically, one could argue that Axl is 50 percent of Guns N' Roses, and with both Malcolm and Phil missing, this felt almost like a Queen + Paul Rodgers situation—even beyond that, with the names reversed.

But at the right end of things, you've got to give Axl huge credit for pulling it off, winning over the fans, convincing thousands of them every night that this wasn't such a bad idea after all. In addition, there's a pretty cool element of going big, going right to the top, with Axl being about the most famous guy that was at all workable. To be sure, purists and music geeks (count me in on both counts), would've loved to have seen Marc Storace from Krokus up there. After all, Dan McCafferty was suffering from his own health issues and couldn't do it, and Doc Neeson, from Australian AC/DC-like legends Angel City, had sadly passed away in 2014 from brain cancer. But yes, ask any deep AC/DC fan and those are the three guys that

would've been perfect choices at various points in time, each being family in some strange way, with each indeed being talked about back when they needed a new lead singer the first time.

Just to dwell on this for a moment (because it's fun), back to this idea of family, each of those feels like a prospective hire similar to that of Stevie Young, which was about the most brilliant replacement for Malcolm that, again, any deep AC/DC fan that was also a music geek would ever want. Once more the theme is family, and again, weirdly perhaps, Dan and Doc—and yes, even Marc Storace—feel like part of the AC/DC family. But instead we got Axl, and a pretty darned brilliant chapter in the band's career got written and nobody went home unsatisfied.

In any event, after the thirteen European shows, the band took the summer off, afterwards conducting a ten-show American leg, commencing August 27, 2016, in Greensboro, North Carolina, and wrapping up September 20 in Philadelphia. And that would be it. Unfortunately, as great as Axl was, it was an untidy end if indeed it's going to be the end at all. The harsh fact is, that wasn't really AC/DC up there. The last AC/DC show as far as many are concerned was February 28 back in Kansas City, Missouri, when Brian was still at the helm, struggling as much as he was.

After it was all over, reprising Coachella, Angus would jump on stage with Guns N' Roses twice in Sydney, Australia, in February 2017, dressed down in jeans and a white T-shirt, attacking the agreed go-to songs "Whole Lotta Rosie" and "Riff Raff." He'd show up once again June 22 of that year in Hanover and then again down the road from his house, July 12, in Goffertpark, Nijmegen, Netherlands, looking very casual playing under bright sunlight, once again in jeans plus a plain gray T-shirt.

All told, a reflective Axl was gracious about his AC/DC experience, calling it both an honor and a personal challenge, also remarking that "Hells Bells" had been the hardest song he'd ever had to perform. He certainly comported himself well during these historic twenty-three shows, to the point where if Brian never returns, there's a clear choice ready to roll if Angus figures he'd like to keep headbanging and knocking knees for a few more precious years. Who knows? Maybe we'll even see Axl on an AC/DC album one day.

Axl Rose and Angus,
onstage at the Volkspark
Arena in Hamburg,
Germany, May 26, 2016

49
THROUGH THE MISTS OF TIME:
REST IN PEACE, GEORGE AND MALCOLM YOUNG

As Phil Rudd once told me, "When it comes to just the feel, George is the feel master. There's just something about George. When he plays bass, he always gets along, like doing it subtly, but he's a fantastic bass player. And, I mean, he did a lot of stuff in Australia with Harry Vanda; back then they had hit after hit after hit after hit. They were just pouring 'em out, and they were great. But it was a little in-house thing, is the way they liked to do it. They weren't a band that was going to come out and show 'em what was going on—they were a radio band. We tried to get George to play bass, for quite a while, in the band. But he had already been through it with The Easybeats and stuff."

On October 22, 2017, AC/DC lost the closest thing they had to a sixth member of the band when mentor, producer, and older brother of Angus and Malcolm, George Young, died at the age of 70. As is to be expected from the very private Young family, cause of death was not specified at the time nor later revealed—in a sense, Phil's assessment of George indicates what he thought about public life.

A band statement on social media read: "It is with pain in our heart that we have to announce the passing of our beloved brother and mentor George Young. Without his help and guidance there would not have been an AC/DC. As a musician, songwriter, producer, advisor and much, much more, you could not ask for a more dedicated and professional man. As a brother, you could not ask for a finer brother. For all he did and gave to us throughout his life, we will always remember him with gratitude and hold him close to our hearts." Added Harry Vanda, co-producer of many of the band's albums with George, "Rest in peace, my dear friend."

Hard to believe, but George's last production for AC/DC had been only three records ago, when he had joined the lads for the making of *Stiff Upper Lip* in Vancouver in 1999, assisted by engineer Mike Fraser, who says the guys had wanted George back on the following album as well. "They had pulled their brother George out of retirement to do *Stiff Upper Lip*, and I think they tried to get him again, and he says, 'Nah, nah, I'm retired; I don't wanna do it.' *Stiff Upper Lip* was a blast to do. They had George, and, oh man, he was such a pleasure to work with. Every one of those takes are completely live. The only thing that is overdubbed would be the vocals and Angus's solos. And the thing is, we would only do three or four takes of each song. They would go and do a take, and it would be like, 'Oh, let's change a few things.' And then they would do another take, 'Now it's getting there.' 'Oh, that's great.' 'Let's do one more.' And you would just really feel it kick in on that one. 'Okay.' [laughs] They'd been a team for so long anyway, just like a big family."

Three weeks after the passing of the first Young brother to become a rock star, another senior member of the family was lost when Malcolm died at Lulworth House in Elizabeth Bay, Sydney, on November 18 at the age of 64. Cause of death was complications due to his severe dementia. His funeral was held ten days later at St. Mary's Cathedral.

In a statement, the family said that "Malcolm Young died peacefully Saturday with his family by his side. Renowned for his musical prowess, Malcolm was a songwriter, guitarist, performer, producer and visionary who inspired many. From the outset, he knew what he wanted to achieve and, along with his younger brother,

took to the world stage giving their all at every show. Nothing less would do for their fans."

The AC/DC organization announced that, "Today it is with deep heartfelt sadness that AC/DC has to announce the passing of Malcolm Young. Malcolm, along with Angus, was the founder and creator of AC/DC. With enormous dedication and commitment he was the driving force behind the band. As a guitarist, songwriter, and visionary he was a perfectionist and a unique man. He always stuck to his guns and did and said exactly what he wanted. He took great pride in all that he endeavored. His loyalty to the fans was unsurpassed."

Final word goes to Angus, who wrote, "As his brother it is hard to express in words what he has meant to me during my life. The bond we had was unique and very special. He leaves behind an enormous legacy that will live on forever. Malcolm, job well done."

Malcolm, 1978

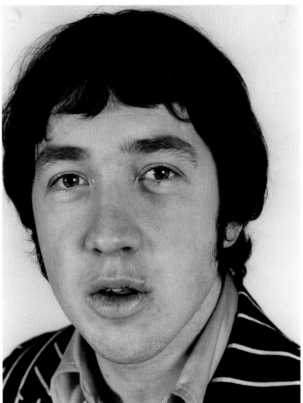

George, 1966

50
FLICK OF THE SWITCH:
SEVENTEENTH ALBUM, *POWER UP*

There's probably no bigger comeback story in all of rock 'n' roll than AC/DC's response to the death of Bon Scott with *Back in Black*. *Power Up* certainly could never compete, but it was both galvanizing and poignant when Angus drew parallels between the two situations (separated by exactly forty years), calling the new record a tribute to Malcolm, just like *Back in Black* was a tribute to Bon.

But there are added dimensions to the present situation that draw the two records closer (notwithstanding that they are both fine AC/DC records, and if *Power Up* is the last we ever hear from the guys, they've left on a high). First, AC/DC have spent the last thirty years as a complicated business juggernaut that, although never disbanded, worked less regularly than most. Many institutions that are of AC/DC's vintage or older toured more on actually slightly less records. Many others made more records and toured more. AC/DC? Well, with respect to bands that never declared that they were broken up (and therefore able to be called reunited), you'd have to put them somewhere in the lower half when it comes to activity across the two categories of new music and playing shows.

I bring this up because the worldwide pandemic turned out to be an excuse for most heritage acts to do nothing, when, logically, they might have replaced greatly reduced touring opportunities with generating *more* new music. And yet AC/DC took the other route. Rather than moan about not being able to work, they went to work and put together what has been deemed "a pandemic album," according to the evolving lexicon of the music biz. In other words, for a band not inclined to work much, AC/DC surprised us with working more than most other aging rockers.

But it goes deeper. *Power Up* also represents a comeback from a near shambles of a situation, given that at various recent points in time, Phil Rudd, Cliff Williams, and Brian Johnson were all out of the band. And yet miraculously, for *Power Up*, all three are part of the backroom poker hand of a band once again, meaning that we've got the exact same AC/DC lineup for two records in a row now.

Providing further continuity, the band recorded once more at The Warehouse in Vancouver with Brendan O'Brien and Mike Fraser, achieving the same sort of plush yet ironically clean sound they'd gotten on the previous four records, with *Rock or Bust* representing a slight anomaly in the form of the sort of unintended clipped distortion most audible at the drums. The sessions lasted six weeks, taking place in August and September 2018, representing a (sensible, not short, not long) time span that is also typical for an AC/DC record.

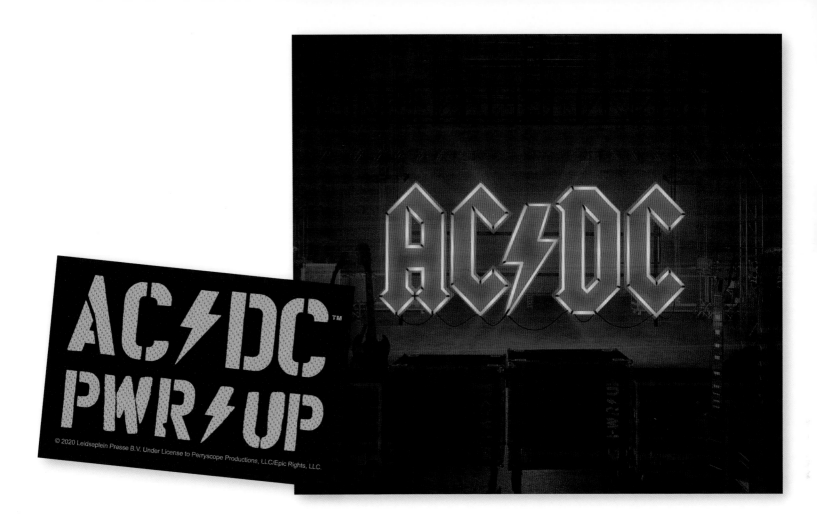

Slight grumbles about the sound notwithstanding, *Power Up* offers a mostly strong set of songs, as well as a longer running time than *Rock or Bust*, although generally in CD circles, forty-one minutes is a scandal. As suspicious tradition, the flagship song from *Power Up* turned out to be the friendly and Stones-y advance single "Shot in the Dark," arriving with much hoopla a month before the album's November 13, 2020, release date. But just as rousing is second single "Realize" and third single "Demon Fire." Meanwhile, "Money Shot," "Code Red," and "Wild Reputation" contribute to the record's variety of tempos, chord sequences, and note densities, with "Through the Mists of Time" (also issued as a single), fulfilling the recent mandate through which the band offers at least one really melodic proposition—these either lean Celtic or southern rock, and this song manages both.

Unfortunately, any excitement over *Power Up* would be short-lived. The album sold appreciably, amassing worldwide sales of 1.4 million units. But the lack of live shows in support of the record meant that once the many reviews of it were registered and read (or watched, or heard), well, AC/DC were now no longer part of the news cycle, and it was back into the pandemic for everybody.

Which is the experience of all of us as I write this, and by all of us, that goes for Brian, Angus, Stevie, Cliff, and Phil as well. Will we ever see AC/DC live again? Will there be more records? If they hit the road again, will it be with someone else leading the party other than Brian?

Only time will tell, but for now, at least we have the pleasure of reporting that the final highlight in this book of fifty career milestones is a happy surprise, in the form of a new full-length album, courtesy of a bunch of crusty old rockers who had no business making one. Perhaps AC/DC will confound expectations once again and return to their proper place in the world, namely that of making millions of people happy by performing—current lineup intact—their many timeless anthems live on huge stages all around the world. With Charlie Watts now gone and the future of The Rolling Stones looking dubious, it just might fall upon Brian and Angus to step up and carry the torch for original, traditional, guitar-charged rock 'n' roll. To be sure, it will need to be passed on soon enough again, but it looks like there's a place of destiny for Brian and Angus in the interim—and that's back participating publicly in the world, taking us to their own land and brand of live rock 'n' roll at its largest and most life-affirmed. Bottom line: The world could sure use an AC/DC concert or two right about now.

DISCOGRAPHY

Concerning a few points on format, I've included an additional notes section for anything I thought was interesting and, er, notable. There are quote marks around songs everywhere except in the track list proper, just to keep things tidy. I present spelling and punctuation of song titles, plus timings and order of the names in the credits, as per Australian release (or "first edition") in the beginning. Although life is still complicated at *Powerage*, that's where I switch over to citing U.S. label and catalog numbers. Even though it's not home territory, America at this point feels most like the headquarters of the official release.

I've noted side 1/side 2 designations for all releases from the vinyl era, which I've always maintained ends in 1990 (trust me, I was there). Information on live albums and compilations is cut back here (writing credits, timings on compilations, etc.). That decision was taken to reduce redundancy, not to mention the fact that many of these albums are discussed in considerable detail elsewhere in the book. Further on the topic of redundancy, I decided against including things like certifications, chart positions, and discussion of singles, which, again, I feel are subjects covered sufficiently throughout our fifty entries.

A. STUDIO ALBUMS

HIGH VOLTAGE

Released February 11, 1975; Albert Productions APLP-009.

Recorded November 1974 at Albert Studios, Sydney, Australia.

Produced by Harry Vanda and George Young.

Side 1: 1. Baby, Please Don't Go 4:50; 2. She's Got Balls 4:51; 3. Little Lover 5:37; 4. Stick Around 4:40.

Side 2: 1. Soul Stripper 6:25; 2. You Ain't Got a Hold on Me 3:31; 3. Love Song 5:15; 4. Show Business 4:46.

All songs composed by Angus Young, Malcolm Young, and Bon Scott except "Baby, Please Don't Go" (Joe Williams) and "Soul Stripper" (Angus Young and Malcolm Young).

Personnel: Bon Scott – lead vocals; Angus Young – lead guitar; Malcolm Young – rhythm guitar, lead guitar, bass guitar, backing vocals; Rob Bailey – bass guitar (in band but limited playing on album); Peter Clack – drums (in band but performs on "Baby, Please Don't Go" only).

Session appearances: George Young – bass guitar, rhythm guitar, backing vocals; Harry Vanda – backing vocals; Tony Currenti – drums (session drummer but plays on all tracks except "Baby, Please Don't Go").

Additional notes: Issued only in Australia. Not to be confused with international versions of *High Voltage*, although "She's Got Balls" and "Little Lover" will be included on those records.

T.N.T.

Released December 1, 1975; Albert Productions APLPA-016.

Recorded March–July 1974 at Albert Studios, Sydney, Australia.

Produced by Harry Vanda and George Young.

Side 1: 1. It's a Long Way to the Top (If You Wanna Rock 'n' Roll) 5:15; 2. The Rock 'n' Roll Singer 5:04; 3. The Jack 5:52; 4. Live Wire 5:49.

Side 2: 1. T.N.T. 3:34; 2. Rocker 2:49; 3. Can I Sit Next to You Girl 4:12; 4. High Voltage 4:02; 5. School Days 5:23.

All songs composed by Angus Young, Malcolm Young, and Bon Scott except "Can I Sit Next to You Girl" (Angus Young and Malcolm Young) and "School Days" (Chuck Berry).

Personnel: Bon Scott – lead vocals, bagpipes; Angus Young – lead guitar; Malcolm Young – rhythm guitar, backing vocals; Mark Evans – bass guitar; Phil Rudd – drums, percussion.

Additional notes: Issued in Australia only; however, the international debut of the band, called *High Voltage*, issued in April 1976 in the United States and the following month in Europe, contains seven of nine tracks, the exceptions being "Rocker" and "School Days." The international *High Voltage* adds two tracks from the Australian issue High Voltage, namely, "She's Got Balls" and "Little Lover."

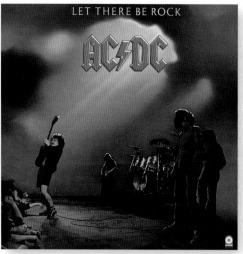

DIRTY DEEDS DONE DIRT CHEAP

Released September 20, 1976; Albert Productions APLP-020.

Recorded December 1975 at Albert Studios, Sydney, Australia, with "Love at First Feel" recorded September 1976 at Vineyard Studios, London, England.

Produced by Harry Vanda and George Young.

Side 1: 1. Dirty Deeds Done Dirt Cheap 4:13; 2. Ain't No Fun (Waiting 'Round to Be a Millionaire) 7:31; 3. There's Gonna Be Some Rockin' 3:17; 4. Problem Child 5:46.

Side 2: 1. Squealer 5:18; 2. Big Balls 2:40; 3. R.I.P. (Rock in Peace) 3:36; 4. Ride On 5:53; 5. Jailbreak 4:41.

All songs composed by Angus Young, Malcolm Young, and Bon Scott.

Personnel: Bon Scott – lead vocals; Angus Young – lead guitar; Malcolm Young – rhythm guitar, backing vocals; Mark Evans – bass guitar; Phil Rudd – drums.

Additional notes: The international version of *Dirty Deeds Done Dirt Cheap* was issued in Europe in 1976 and in the United States and Canada in 1981. The international version deletes "R.I.P. (Rock in Peace)" and "Jailbreak" and adds "Rocker" (from the Australian album T.N.T.) and "Love at First Feel," a track not included on any of the band's Australian albums.

LET THERE BE ROCK

Released March 21, 1977; Albert Productions APLP-022.

Recorded January–February 1977 at Albert Studios, Sydney, Australia.

Produced by Harry Vanda and George Young.

Side 1: 1. Go Down 5:17; 2. Dog Eat Dog 3:30; 3. Let There Be Rock 6:02; 4. Bad Boy Boogie 4:18.

Side 2: 1. Overdose 5:47; 2. Crabsody in Blue 4:39; 3. Hell Ain't a Bad Place to Be 4:12; 4. Whole Lotta Rosie 5:25.

All songs composed by Angus Young, Malcolm Young, and Bon Scott.

Personnel: Bon Scott – lead vocals; Angus Young – lead guitar; Malcolm Young – rhythm guitar, backing vocals; Mark Evans – bass guitar; Phil Rudd – drums, percussion.

Additional notes: The U.S., Canadian, and Japanese versions of *Let There Be Rock* delete "Crabsody in Blue" and add "Problem Child" from *Dirty Deeds Done Dirt Cheap*.

POWERAGE

Released May 5, 1978; Atlantic SD 19180.

Recorded February–March 1978 at Albert Studios, Sydney, Australia.

Produced by Harry Vanda and George Young.

Side 1: 1. Rock 'n' Roll Damnation 3:35; 2. Down Payment Blues 6:20; 3. Gimme a Bullet 3:00; 4. Riff Raff 5:14.

Side 2: 1. Sin City 4:40; 2. What's Next to the Moon 3:15; 3. Gone Shootin' 4:05; 4. Up to My Neck in You 4:58; 5. Kicked in the Teeth 3:45.

All songs composed by Angus Young, Malcolm Young, and Bon Scott.

Personnel: Bon Scott – lead vocals; Angus Young – guitar; Malcolm Young – guitar; Cliff Williams – bass; Phil Rudd – drums.

Additional notes: The European version of *Powerage* features an earlier mix than the subsequent U.S., Canadian, and Australian mixes, including minor performance differences. Initial European copies of *Powerage* included "Cold Hearted Man" but not "Rock 'n' Roll Damnation." Later issues contained both. Australian, U.S., and Canadian issues included "Rock 'n' Roll Damnation" but not "Cold Hearted Man." *Powerage* was the first AC/DC album where the cover art was the same across all territories.

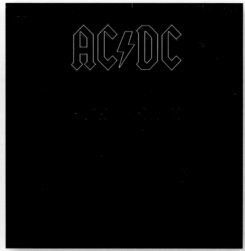

HIGHWAY TO HELL

Released July 27, 1979; Atlantic SD 19244.

Recorded March–April 1979 at Roundhouse Studios, London, England, with additional work at Albert Studios, Sydney, Australia, and Criteria Studios, Miami, Florida.

Produced by Robert John Lange.

Side 1: 1. Highway to Hell 3:26; 2. Girls Got Rhythm 3:23; 3. Walk All Over You 5:08; 4. Touch Too Much 4:24; 5. Beating Around the Bush 3:55.

Side 2: 1. Shot Down in Flames 3:21; 2. Get It Hot 2:24; 3. If You Want Blood (You've Got It) 4:32; 4. Love Hungry Man 4:14; 5. Night Prowler 6:13.

All songs composed by Angus Young, Malcolm Young, and Bon Scott.

Personnel: Bon Scott – lead vocals; Angus Young – guitar; Malcolm Young – guitar; Cliff Williams – bass; Phil Rudd – drums.

BACK IN BLACK

Released July 25, 1980; Atlantic SD 16018.

Recorded April–May 1980 at Compass Point Studios, Nassau, Bahamas.

Produced by Robert John "Mutt" Lange.

Side 1: 1. Hells Bells 5:10; 2. Shoot to Thrill 5:17; 3. What Do You Do for Money Honey 3:36; 4. Given the Dog a Bone 3:31; 5. Let Me Put My Love into You 4:12.

Side 2: 1. Back in Black 4:17; 2. You Shook Me All Night Long 3:29; 3. Have a Drink on Me 4:01; 4. Shake a Leg 4:04; 5. Rock and Roll Ain't Noise Pollution 4:13.

All songs composed by Angus Young, Malcolm Young, and Brian Johnson.

Personnel: Brian Johnson – lead vocals; Angus Young – lead guitar; Malcolm Young – rhythm guitar, backing vocals; Cliff Williams – bass guitar, backing vocals; Phil Rudd – drums.

FOR THOSE ABOUT TO ROCK

Released November 23, 1981; Atlantic SD 11111.

Recorded August–September 1981 on Mobile One at H.I.S. Studio, Paris, France, and Family Studio, Paris, France.

Produced by Robert John "Mutt" Lange.

Side 1: 1. For Those About to Rock (We Salute You) 5:44; 2. Put the Finger on You 3:25; 3. Let's Get It Up 3:54; 4. Inject the Venom 3:30; 5. Snowballed 3:23.

Side 2: 1. Evil Walks 4:24; 2. C.O.D. 3:19; 3. Breaking the Rules 4:23; 4. Night of the Long Knives 3:26; 5. Spellbound 4:30.

All songs composed by Angus Young, Malcolm Young, and Brian Johnson.

Personnel: Brian Johnson – lead vocals; Angus Young – lead guitar; Malcolm Young – rhythm guitar, backing vocals; Cliff Williams – bass guitar, backing vocals; Phil Rudd – drums.

FLICK OF THE SWITCH

Released August 15, 1983; Atlantic 80100-1.

Recorded April 1983 at Compass Point Studios, Nassau, Bahamas.

Produced by AC/DC.

Side 1: 1. Rising Power 3:39; 2. This House Is on Fire 3:22; 3. Flick of the Switch 3:09; 4. Nervous Shakedown 4:23; 5. Landslide 3:55.

Side 2: 1. Guns for Hire 3:28; 2. Deep in the Hole 3:25; 3. Bedlam in Belgium 3:48; 4. Badlands 3:34; 5. Brain Shake 3:54.

All songs composed by Angus Young, Malcolm Young, and Brian Johnson.

Personnel: Brian Johnson – lead vocals; Angus Young – lead guitar; Malcolm Young – rhythm guitar, backing vocals; Cliff Williams – bass guitar, backing vocals; Phil Rudd – drums.

FLY ON THE WALL

Released June 28, 1985; Atlantic 81263-1.

Recorded October 1984–February 1985 at Mountain Studios, Montreux, Switzerland.

Produced by Angus Young and Malcolm Young.

Side 1: 1. Fly on the Wall 3:44; 2. Shake Your Foundations 4:10; 3. First Blood 3:46; 4. Danger 4:22.

Side 2: 1. Playing with Girls 3:44; 2. Stand Up 3:53; 3. Hell or High Water 4:32; 4. Back in Business 4:24; 5. Send for the Man 3:36.

All songs composed by Angus Young, Malcolm Young, and Brian Johnson.

Personnel: Brian Johnson – lead vocals; Angus Young – lead guitar; Malcolm Young – rhythm guitar, backing vocals; Cliff Williams – bass guitar, backing vocals; Simon Wright – drums, percussion.

BLOW UP YOUR VIDEO

Released January 18, 1988; Atlantic 81828-1.

Recorded August–September 1987 at Miraval Studio, Le Val, Provence, France.

Produced by Harry Vanda and George Young.

Side 1: 1. Heatseeker 3:50; 2. That's the Way I Wanna Rock 'n' Roll 3:45; 3. Meanstreak 4:08; 4. Go Zone 4:26; 5. Kissin' Dynamite 3:58.

Side 2: 1. Nick of Time 4:16; 2. Some Sin for Nuthin' 4:11, 3. Ruff Stuff 4:28; 4. Two's Up 5:19; 5. This Means War 4:21.

All songs composed by Angus Young and Malcolm Young.

Personnel: Brian Johnson – lead vocals; Angus Young – lead guitar; Malcolm Young – rhythm guitar, backing vocals; Cliff Williams – bass guitar, backing vocals; Simon Wright – drums, percussion.

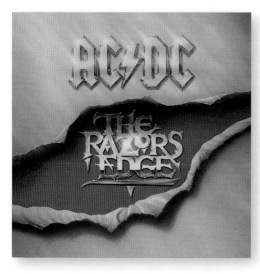

THE RAZORS EDGE

Released September 21, 1990; ATCO 7 91413-2.

Recorded March–May 1990 at Windmill Road Studios, Dublin, Ireland, and Little Mountain Studios, Vancouver, British Columbia, Canada.

Produced by Bruce Fairbairn.

1. Thunderstruck 4:52; 2. Fire Your Guns 2:53; 3. Moneytalks 3:48; 4. The Razors Edge 4:22; 5. Mistress for Christmas 3:59; 6. Rock Your Heart Out 4:06; 7. Are You Ready 4:10; 8. Got You by the Balls 4:30; 9. Shot of Love 3:56; 10. Let's Make It 3:32; 11. Goodbye & Good Riddance to Bad Luck 3:13; 12. If You Dare 3:08.

All songs composed by Angus Young and Malcolm Young.

Personnel: Brian Johnson – lead vocals; Angus Young – lead guitar; Malcolm Young – rhythm guitar, backing vocals; Cliff Williams – bass guitar, backing vocals; Chris Slade – drums, percussion.

BALLBREAKER

Released September 26, 1995; EastWest 61780-1.

Recorded 1994–March 1995 at The Record Plant, New York, NY, and Ocean Way Studios, Los Angeles, California.

Produced by Rick Rubin; co-produced by Mike Fraser.

1. Hard as a Rock 4:31; 2. Cover You in Oil 4:32; 3. The Furor 4:10; 4. Boogie Man 4:07; 5. The Honey Roll 5:34; 6. Burnin' Alive 5:05; 7. Hail Caesar 5:14; 8. Love Bomb 3:14; 9. Caught with Your Pants Down 4:14; 10. Whiskey on the Rocks 4:35; 11. Ballbreaker 4:31.

All songs composed by Angus Young and Malcolm Young.

Personnel: Brian Johnson – lead vocals; Angus Young – rhythm and lead guitars; Malcolm Young – rhythm guitar, backing vocals; Cliff Williams – bass guitar, backing vocals; Phil Rudd – drums, percussion.

STIFF UPPER LIP

Released February 28, 2000; EastWest 62494-2.

Recorded September–October 1999 at The Warehouse Studio, Vancouver, British Columbia, Canada.

Produced by George Young.

1. Stiff Upper Lip 3:34; 2. Meltdown 3:41; 3. House of Jazz 3:56; 4. Hold Me Back 3:59; 5. Safe in New York City 3:59; 6. Can't Stand Still 3:41; 7. Can't Stop Rock 'n' Roll 4:02; 8. Satellite Blues 3:46; 9. Damned 3:52; 10. Come and Get It 4:02; 11. All Screwed Up 4:36; 12. Give It Up 3:54.

All songs composed by Angus Young and Malcolm Young.

Personnel: Brian Johnson – lead vocals; Angus Young – lead guitar; Malcolm Young – rhythm guitar, backing vocals; Cliff Williams – bass guitar, backing vocals; Phil Rudd – drums.

BLACK ICE

Released October 20, 2008; Columbia 88697383771.

Recorded March 3–April 25, 2008, at The Warehouse Studio, Vancouver, British Columbia, Canada.

Produced by Brendan O'Brien.

1. Rock N Roll Train 4:21; 2. Skies on Fire 3:34; 3. Big Jack 3:57; 4. Anything Goes 3:22; 5. War Machine 3:09; 6. Smash 'n' Grab 4:06; 7. Spoilin' for a Fight 3:17; 8. Wheels 3:28; 9. Decibel 3:34; 10: Stormy May Day 3:10; 1. She Likes Rock N Roll 3:53; 12. Money Made 4:15; 13. Rock N Roll Dream 4:41; 14. Rocking All the Way 3:22; 15. Black Ice 3:25.

All songs composed by Angus Young and Malcolm Young.

Personnel: Brian Johnson – lead vocals; Angus Young – lead guitar, slide guitar; Malcolm Young – rhythm guitar, backing vocals; Cliff Williams – bass guitar, backing vocals; Phil Rudd – drums, percussion.

ROCK OR BUST

Released November 28, 2014; Columbia 88875034852.

Recorded May 3–July 12, 2014, at The Warehouse Studio, Vancouver, British Columbia, Canada.

Produced by Brendan O'Brien.

1. Rock or Bust 3:03; 2. Play Ball 2:47; 3. Rock the Blues Away 3:24; 4. Miss Adventure 2:57; 5. Dogs of War 3:35; 6. Got Some Rock & Roll Thunder 3:22; 7. Hard Times 2:44; 8. Baptism of Fire 3:30; 9. Rock the House 2:42; 10. Sweet Candy 3:09; 11. Emission Control 3:41.

All songs composed by Angus Young and Malcolm Young.

Personnel: Brian Johnson – lead vocals; Angus Young – lead guitar; Stevie Young – rhythm guitar, backing vocals; Cliff Williams – bass guitar, backing vocals; Phil Rudd – drums; guest performance: Brendan O'Brien – backing vocals.

POWER UP

Released November 13, 2020; Columbia 19439725561.

Recorded August–September 2018 and early 2019 at The Warehouse, Vancouver, British Columbia, Canada.

Produced by Brendan O'Brien.

1. Realize 3:37; 2. Rejection 4:06; 3. Shot in the Dark 3:06; 4. Through the Mists of Time 3:32; 5. Kick You When You're Down 3:10; 6. Witch's Spell 3:42; 7. Demon Fire 3:30; 8. Wild Reputation 2:54; 9. No Man's Land 3:39; 10. Systems Down 3:12; 11. Money Shot 3:05; 12. Code Red 3:31.

All songs composed by Angus Young and Malcolm Young.

Personnel: Brian Johnson – lead vocals; Angus Young – lead guitar; Stevie Young – rhythm guitar, backing vocals; Cliff Williams – bass guitar, backing vocals; Phil Rudd – drums.

B.
LIVE ALBUMS

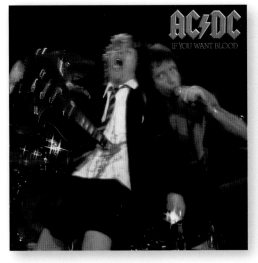

IF YOU WANT BLOOD

Released October 13, 1978; Atlantic SD 19212.

Recorded mostly on April 30, 1978, at the Apollo Theatre, Glasgow, United Kingdom.

Produced by Harry Vanda and George Young.

Side 1: 1. Riff Raff 5:10; 2. Hell Ain't a Bad Place to Be 4:02; 3. Bad Boy Boogie 7:35; 4. The Jack 5:43.

Side 2: 1. Whole Lotta Rosie 3:50; 2. Rock 'n' Roll Damnation 3:30; 3. High Voltage 6:00; 4. Let There Be Rock 8:15; 5. Rocker 3:00.

Personnel: Bon Scott – lead vocals; Angus Young – guitar; Malcolm Young – guitar; Cliff Williams – bass; Phil Rudd – drums.

LIVE

Released October 27, 1992; Atlantic 92215-2.

Recorded April 23–September 28, 1991.

Produced by Bruce Fairbairn.

1. Thunderstruck 6:34; 2. Shoot to Thrill 5:21; 3. Back in Black 4:28; 4. Who Made Who 5:15; 5. Heatseeker 3:37; 6. The Jack 6:56; 7. Moneytalks 4:18; 8. Hells Bells 6:01; 9. Dirty Deeds Done Dirt Cheap 5:02; 10. Whole Lotta Rosie 4:30; 11. You Shook Me All Night Long 3:54; 12. Highway to Hell 3:58; 13. T.N.T. 3:47; 14. For Those About to Rock (We Salute You) 7:09.

Personnel: Brian Johnson – lead vocals; Angus Young – lead guitar; Malcolm Young – rhythm guitar, backing vocals; Cliff Williams – bass guitar, backing vocals; Chris Slade – drums, percussion.

Additional notes: Also available in a two-CD Collector's Edition and a two-LP vinyl Collector's Edition.

LIVE AT RIVER PLATE

Released November 19, 2012; Columbia 88765 41175 2.

Recorded December 2, 4, 6, 2009, at River Plate Stadium, Buenos Aires, Argentina.

Produced by Rocky Oldham.

CD1: 1. Rock N Roll Train 4:41; 2. Hell Ain't a Bad Place to Be 4:27; 3. Back in Black 4:15; 4. Big Jack 4:07; 5. Dirty Deeds Done Dirt Cheap 4:58; 6. Shot Down in Flames 3:47; 7. Thunderstruck 5:32; 8. Black Ice 3:44; 9. The Jack 10:12; 10. Hells Bells 5:37.

CD2: 1. Shoot to Thrill; 2. War Machine 3:39; 3. Dog Eat Dog 5:09; 4. You Shook Me All Night Long 4:01; 5. T.N.T. 3:57; 6. Whole Lotta Rosie 5:57; 7. Let There Be Rock 18:06; 8. Highway to Hell 4:44; 9. For Those About to Rock (We Salute You) 7:45.

Personnel: Brian Johnson – lead vocals; Angus Young – lead guitar, slide guitar; Malcolm Young – rhythm guitar, backing vocals; Cliff Williams – bass guitar, backing vocals; Phil Rudd – drums, percussion

Additional notes: Also available on DVD, Blu-Ray, and vinyl.

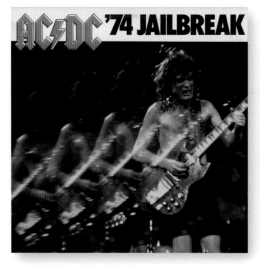

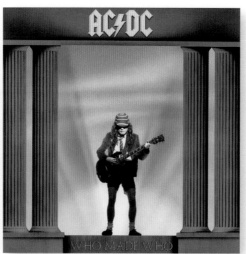

'74 JAILBREAK

Released October 15, 1984; Atlantic 80178-1.

Side 1: 1. Jailbreak; 2. You Ain't Got a Hold on Me; 3. Show Business.

Side 2: 1. Soul Stripper; 2. Baby, Please Don't Go.

Additional notes: EP of early-days songs previously available only on Australian releases.

WHO MADE WHO

Released May 24, 1986; Atlantic 81650-1

Side 1: 1. Who Made Who; 2. You Shook Me All Night Long; 3. D.T.; 4. Sink the Pink; 5. Ride On.

Side 2: 1. Hells Bells; 2. Shake Your Foundations; 3. Chase the Ace; 4. For Those About to Rock (We Salute You).

Additional notes: Soundtrack compilation album consisting of six previously released songs and three new tracks written for the Maximum Overdrive movie.

IRON MAN 2

Released April 19, 2010; Columbia 88697 60952 2.

1. Shoot to Thrill; 2. Rock 'n' Roll Damnation; 3. Guns for Hire; 4. Cold Hearted Man; 5. Back in Black; 6. Thunderstruck; 7. If You Want Blood (You've Got It); 8. Evil Walks; 9. T.N.T.; 10. Hell Ain't a Bad Place to Be; 11. Have a Drink on Me; 12. The Razors Edge; 13. Let There Be Rock; 14. War Machine; 15. Highway to Hell.

Additional Notes: Compilation album for the movie. Deluxe version includes a (mostly) live DVD. Also issued on double vinyl.

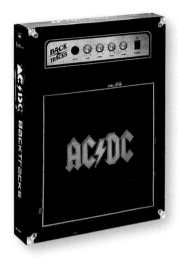

BONFIRE

Released November 18, 1997; EastWest 62119-2.

CD1: 1. Live Wire; 2. Problem Child;
3. High Voltage; 4. Hell Ain't a Bad Place to
Be; 5. Dog Eat Dog; 6. The Jack; 7. Whole Lotta
Rosie; 8. Rocker.

CD2: 1. Live Wire; 2. Shot Down in Flames;
3. Hell Ain't a Bad Place to Be; 4. Sin City;
5. Walk All Over You; 6. Bad Boy Boogie.

CD3: 1. The Jack; 2. Highway to Hell; 3. Girls
Got Rhythm; 4. High Voltage; 5. Whole Lotta
Rosie; 6. Rocker; 7. T.N.T.; 8. Let There Be
Rock.

CD4: 1. Dirty Eyes; 2. Touch Too Much;
3. If You Want Blood You Got It; 4. Back
Seat Confidential; 5. Get It Hot; 6. Sin City;
7. She's Got Balls; 8. School Days;
9. It's a Long Way to the Top if You Wanna
Rock 'n' Roll; 10. Ride On.

CD5: 1. Hells Bells; 2. Shoot to Thrill; 3. What
Do You Do for Money Honey; 4. Given the
Dog a Bone; 5. Let Me Put My Love into You;
6. Back in Black; 7. You Shook Me All Night
Long; 8. Have a Drink on Me; 9. Shake a Leg;
10. Rock and Roll Ain't Noise Pollution.

Additional notes: CD1 is *Live from the Atlantic
Studios*, CD2 and CD3 are *Let There Be Rock:
The Movie, Live in Paris*, CD4 is the Volts
rarities CD, and CD5 is *Back in Black*.

BACKTRACKS

Released November 10, 2009; Columbia
88697540982.

CD1: 1. Stick Around; 2. Love Song;
3. Fling Thing; 4. R.I.P. (Rock in Peace);
5. Carry Me Home; 6. Crabsody in Blue;
7. Cold Hearted Man; 8. Snake Eye;
9. Borrowed Time; 10. Down on the
Borderline; 11. Big Gun; 12. Cyberspace

CD2: 1. Dirty Deeds Done Dirt Cheap;
2. Dog Eat Dog; 3. Live Wire; 4. Shot Down
in Flames; 5. Back in Black; 6. T.N.T.;
7. Let There Be Rock; 8. Guns for Hire;
9. Rock and Roll Ain't Noise Pollution;
10. This House Is on Fire; 11. You Shook Me
All Night Long; 12. Jailbreak; 13. Highway to
Hell; 14. For Those About to Rock (We Salute
You); 15. Safe in New York City.

Additional notes: The tracks on CD2 are all
live. In the spirit of this being a discography
and not a videography, I've not listed the tracks
for the DVD; but yes, there's a full-length
DVD of videos as well. Deluxe Edition
includes a second DVD and different CD
tracks. There's also a vinyl edition that culls
the studio rarities only.

INDEX

IMAGE CREDITS

A = all, B = bottom, L = left, M = middle,
R = right, T = top

Alamy Stock Photos: 10, Pictorial Press; 33, Goddard Archive Portraits; 35TR, Goddard Archive Portraits; 39BL, Pictorial Press; 46, Sheri Lynn Behr; 51T, Pictorial Press; 52–53, Sheri Lynn Behr; 54R, Sheri Lynn Behr; 55L, Sheri Lynn Behr; 62, Pictorial Press; 65L, Media Punch; 65R, The Picture Art Collection; 66, Mirrorpix; 76, Album; 87B, Mirrorpix; 94, Mirrorpix; 95, Mirrorpix; 96, Mirrorpix; 103, Media Punch; 104–105, Media Punch; 106-107, Mirrorpix; 131, Pictorial Press Ltd; 132R, Simon Meaker; 133, Simon Meaker; 137, REUTERS; 142, REUTERS; 144, REUTERS; 145, Scott Weiner/MediaPunch Inc; 146B, Martyn Goddard; 147T, Martyn Goddard; 147BL, Martyn Goddard; 147B, Martyn Goddard; 147BR, Martyn Goddard; 148, WENN Rights Ltd; 152, WENN Rights Ltd; 153, Gonzales Photo; 156-157, REUTERS; 160-161, ZUMA Press Inc; 167, ZUMA Press Inc; 168-169, dpa picture alliance; 171BL, Pictorial Press Ltd; 171BR, Pictorial Press Ltd; 172-173, Martin Berry.

AP Images: 120, 121, 150.

Getty Images: 2, Dick Barnatt/Redferns; 16L, GAB Archive/Redferns; 19, WEA/ ullstein bild; 26–27, Dick Barnatt/Redferns; 28–29, Michael Putland/Hulton Archive; 37, Jorgen Angel/Redferns; 41, Fin Costello/ Redferns; 42, Michael Ochs Archives; 43TL, Michael Ochs Archives; 43TR, Linda D. Robbins/Hulton Archive; 51B, Paul Natkin; 67L, Mirrorpix; 69T, Ron Pownall/Corbis Historical; 69B, Watal Asanuma/Shinko Music/Hulton Archive; 77, Michael Putland/ Hulton Archive; 78, Midori Tsukagoshi/ Shinko Music/Hulton Archive; 82, Midori Tsukagoshi/Shinko Music/Hulton Archive; 83B, Clayton Call/Redferns; 88B, Michael Ochs Archives; 91B, Michael Ochs Archives; 98, Michael Ochs Archives; 99, Ebet Roberts/ Redferns; 100, Ebet Roberts/Redferns; 109T, Bob King/Redferns; 109BR, Icon and Image/Michael Ochs Archives; 110, Bob King/Redferns; 113, Steve Rapport/Hulton Archive; 116–117, Mick Hutson/Redferns; 119T, Michael Ochs Archives; 125T, Larry Hulst/ Michael Ochs Archives; 127, Martin Goodacre/ Hulton Archive; 138, KMazur/WireImage; 139, KMazur/WireImage; 141, Kevin Kane/ WireImage; 143, KMazur/WireImage; 154BL, Ullstein Bld; 155T, JP Yim; 159, REUTERS; 165, Jason Squires/WireImage; 192, Rob Verhorst/Redferns.

Martin Popoff Collection: 7, 9A, 39BR, 47BR, 61BL, 61BR, 81BR, 85TL, 85BL, 86A, 87TL, 87TR, 92TR, 92BR, 101, 103BR, 122, 123T, 123B, 129TR, 134T, 136, 163BL, 163BR.

Mike Milsom: 122.

Philip Morris: 12, 14, 15, 22-23, 24, 25L.

Robert Alford: 5, 56–57, 58–59, 71, 72–73.

Robert Barry: 44–45A.

Rock `N` Roll Comics/Courtesy of Re-Visionary Press and the Shapiro Family: 13TR, 67BR.

Wyco Vintage: 109M, 119B.

All memorabilia from the Quarto Publishing archive, unless noted.

Brimming with creative inspiration, how-to projects, and useful information to enrich your everyday life, quarto.com is a favorite destination for those pursuing their interests and passions.

Inspiring | Educating | Creating | Entertaining

© 2023 Quarto Publishing Group USA Inc.
Text © 2023 Martin Popoff

First Published in 2023 by Motorbooks, an imprint of The Quarto Group,
100 Cummings Center, Suite 265-D, Beverly, MA 01915, USA.
T (978) 282-9590 F (978) 283-2742
Quarto.com

All rights reserved. No part of this book may be reproduced in any form without written permission of the copyright owners. All images in this book have been reproduced with the knowledge and prior consent of the artists concerned, and no responsibility is accepted by producer, publisher, or printer for any infringement of copyright or otherwise, arising from the contents of this publication. Every effort has been made to ensure that credits accurately comply with information supplied. We apologize for any inaccuracies that may have occurred and will resolve inaccurate or missing information in a subsequent reprinting of the book.

This book has not been prepared or approved by AC/DC or any of its individual members past or present. This is an unofficial publication.

Motorbooks titles are also available at discount for retail, wholesale, promotional, and bulk purchase. For details, contact the Special Sales Manager by email at specialsales@quarto.com or by mail at The Quarto Group, Attn: Special Sales Manager, 100 Cummings Center, Suite 265-D, Beverly, MA 01915, USA.

26 25 24 23 22   1 2 3 4 5

ISBN: 978-0-7603-7741-3

Digital edition published in 2023
eISBN: 978-0-7603-7742-0

Library of Congress Cataloging-in-Publication Data

Names: Popoff, Martin, 1963- author.
Title: AC/DC at 50 / Martin Popoff.
Other titles: AC/DC at fifty
Description: Beverly, MA : Motorbooks, 2023. | Includes index. | Summary: "Authored by acclaimed rock writer Martin Popoff, AC/DC at 50 provides a
  visually stunning and authoritative celebration of the legendary Aussie
  rockers on their 50th anniversary"-- Provided by publisher.
Identifiers: LCCN 2022037106 | ISBN 9780760377413 | ISBN 9780760377420
  (ebook)
Subjects: LCSH: AC/DC (Musical group) | Rock
  musicians--Australia--Biography. | Rock music--Australia--History and
  criticism.
Classification: LCC ML421.A28 P68 2023 | DDC
  782.42166092/2--dc23/eng/20220804
LC record available at https://lccn.loc.gov/2022037106

Design: Burge Agency
Cover Image: Gonzales Photo/Alamy Stock Photo
Page Layout: Burge Agency

Printed in China